FOREWORD

This book helps to define what it means to be responsible to people with substantial disabilities by focusing attention on them as choice makers.

Increased consciousness of choice disturbs confidence in current service arrangements for people with substantial disabilities. Looking at typical practice from the perspective of opportunities to select from among meaningful alternatives discloses many services as structured to keep groups of people waiting for things to happen to them, and many relationships with staff as inadequate to elicit and support the range of preferences that express individual identity. Quieting this disturbance has been simple, requiring no more than the assertion that some people are too severely disabled to express preferences or appreciate differences, or the claim that the costs of accommodating choice are unmanageable. Those whose work this book reflects decided against these easy ways out and their work gives us many interesting ways into the complexities of choice for people who challenge our abilities to understand them and require substantial assistance to define and implement their choices.

The projects, whose two years of practical work yields the lessons presented here, explored people's choices in multiple contexts including expanding friendships, engaging in everyday community activities, trying jobs in ordinary workplaces, moving from school into an adult life that remembers and reflects personal interests and capacities, and joining with knowledgeable advocates to gain respect for human rights and to achieve adequate services. These contexts frame the question of choice ambitiously because they include increasing people's influence over conditions within their existing service arrangements, but move far beyond this worthwhile but limited objective. Indeed, the lessons from these projects challenge the assumptions at the foundation of most services for people with substantial disabilities.

Discovering and honouring people's choices in new contexts calls for important and difficult changes. Both those choosing and those assisting choice assume new risks and face new uncertainties as they explore new roles and new responsibilities. Unless those involved can build relationships strong enough to create the trust and the communication flows necessary to negotiate the necessary flexibility to learn new ways, opportunities for choice will be stunted and so will people's lives. These projects demonstrate that the keys to the relationships that underpin choice will not be found in a toolkit of professional techniques, but in the willingness to thoughtfully share time, respectfully moving back and forth from familiar to different in a rhythm that, at different moments, gives the person with a disability both the sense of being in charge and the sense of being invited and supported into new opportunities. Finding and keeping a rhythm that matches each person may require many adaptations and call on people with disabilities to be resilient and forgiving when their assistants drop the beat.

These projects demonstrate that many people with substantial disabilities respond to project workers' interest in knowing them, accepting direction from them, and walking with them to open new possibilities. Over time, a number of people responded to project workers with trust and generosity, finding ways to share their interests and preferences with workers as they tried new things together. The growth of relationships between project workers and the people they have met is notable, given that a number of people live and spend their days in situations that offer them little opportunity for individual expression or control of their daily lives. That it took time to build these relationships is no surprise.

Reflecting on the work reported here, readers can only avoid questioning their own deepest assumptions about people with substantial disabilities by resorting to the self-fulfilling excuse that "the people I work with are much more disabled than the people in these projects". The burden of these projects' learning refutes this lazy dodge. There is no doubt that each reader holds a place in the lives of people who are unique individuals who may require imaginative and faithful efforts to assist them to find their own ways to discover and communicate their identity. There is also no doubt that no one can claim to care, who tolerates people's disappearance into being one of a group with little opportunity to form new relationships and explore the responsibilities and rewards of choice. Substantial disability has too often provided the excuse for people's disappearance. As all those who did the work reported here now, this excuse can never be valid.

John O'Brien

Affiliated to the Centre on Human Policy at Syracuse University, the National Development Team, and the Canadian Centre for Integrated Education and Community

A PERSONAL VIEW OF CHOICE

People usually get to make more choices as they grow up because parents and others can trust them more, but people with learning disabilities don't always get this trust and these choices.

Some severely disabled people get no choices – about where to go, what to do, what to wear, when to go to bed... All these things are decided for them, without consulting them.

Really very few people are so disabled that they can't make any choices, if they are given the opportunity.

Choice is important to us; it may be a nuisance having to make our minds up, but it is a great deal better than having our minds made up by someone else... or other people pretending that we don't have a mind that we could make up.

Sit down at bedtime and count how many choices you have made that day. Then think about what it would have been like if all those choices had been denied you.

Most choices are personal day-to-day choices, but people with learning disabilities also expect to be involved in other choices; for example, choosing their local councillors.

In services, people are now expecting the right to help choose staff. Nationally, they are helping to choose the priorities for the government's new Learning Disability Strategy.

So where once people were frozen out, now they are inside and deciding things for themselves.

My most important choices? Well, to work for Mencap as a volunteer... to be involved with Inclusion Europe, to go on holiday somewhere... and to support my local football team.

L. D. Page

Lloyd Page

Vice-President, The European Committee of Inclusion International

CONTENTS

Chapter 1

The choice
initiative

INTRODUCTION

> I would like a chance to try out different things and then choose what I want.
> *(Mental Health Foundation, 1996a: 41)*

The Choice Initiative has its roots in the Mental Health Foundation's Committee of Inquiry into Opportunities and Services for People with a Learning Disability. The evidence sent to the Committee and the subsequent report, *Building Expectations* (1996a), underlined the importance of choice.

The accessible version of *Building Expectations,* written by Change, an organisation for people with learning disabilities and additional sensory impairments, reaffirmed the pre-eminence of choice:

> There needs to be choices in services for people with learning disabilities. As they get older and get more skills, they need new choices and things to do.
> *(Mental Health Foundation, 1996b: 26)*

Similarly, members of the Camden Society for People with Learning Disabilities expressed their wishes in the *Building Expectations* video:

> I would like to go country dancing please... I would like more outings from college.
> *(Mental Health Foundation, 1997)*

Despite these clearly articulated wishes, *Building Expectations* painted a picture of limited choice, in which varied opportunities were only open to a minority:

> Most people continue to lead very restricted lives, waiting for things to happen to them. *(Mental Health Foundation, 1996a: 16)*

The Inquiry's main focus was on the experiences of people who could express themselves in words, while acknowledging that:

> It is our view that whatever the nature of the disability... the central issue is the need for services to be tailored to individual circumstances... We have not been able to analyse to the same extent the additional needs of people with profound and multiple disabilities. *(Mental Health Foundation, 1996a: 16)*

In the light of this, the Foundation decided to follow up the Inquiry by exploring specifically the way in which those with severe, profound and multiple learning disabilities who had high support needs could be empowered to make choices.

With the support of the Henry Smith Charity and the European Social Fund GB, the Foundation established the Choice Initiative with a programme of five innovative projects. Over two years, they explored the ways in which people with high support needs could make their wishes known and bring changes to their lives.

From personal experience, I knew that it was important to listen to people who never use words and find ways to give them control over their lives. But I also knew that this was not easy. My younger son, Peter, in the 18 years of his life, never used speech. He expressed himself by gesture and sound; he would also fetch objects such as plates, a mug, crisps, and his cassette recorder. He could use a couple of Makaton signs, especially the one for please, which he believed was the key to making things happen for him. We began to use photos and made an album of people and places in his life. We showed them to him when changes were going to occur and were planning to develop their use so that he, in his turn, could indicate options.

Sometimes, though, we could not understand what Peter was telling us. At other times, we could not comply; for example, having finished the first meal after moving house, he went to collect his coat, presumably because he thought we were going back to the house he knew. He could become frustrated and distressed when unable to communicate or when he felt his wishes were being ignored. As he approached school-leaving age, we worried about the further limitations on his opportunities.

Other family carers echo my worries. A mother whose son was participating in one of the Choice Initiative projects told me how very pleased she was that the Foundation was focusing on adults with high support needs as she felt they were neglected.

In setting up the Choice Initiative, the Foundation believed that a programme of innovative projects could unlock some of the doors to communication and choice for people with high support needs.

According to the advertised funding criteria, participants in the projects were to have high support needs, and in particular, little or no verbal communication. Over a two to three year period, the projects would focus on supporting people to express their preferences and to bring about changes in their lives, either in daytime opportunities, leisure, housing or friendships.

The Choice Initiative was not intended to be a formal piece of research, but a series of innovative service development projects, whose progress would be monitored and findings evaluated. The Foundation received over 300 enquiries – more than in any other previous grant-giving round – and 64 completed applications. Maybe this reflects the fact that our concern for choice was widely shared; maybe it also reflects a general lack of resources.

Assumptions about choice

In focusing on choice we were working from the premise that it is of crucial importance. We valued choice in our own lives and believed it to be a universal right. At a subsequent workshop on choice for project staff held at the Foundation, Paul Hocker, one of the group, reflected on how far following up preferences is taken for granted by most people.

That night, I thought a bit about the number of small day-to-day choices I made and how I made them. They just happened and required little attention or review. I had never questioned my right to make choices and at times even resented the responsibility of freedom... Years of having the opportunity to make choices had produced a tried and tested recipe for the big issues. A structured process of weighing up pros and cons, mixing in my own experience, adding a generous dash of other people's viewpoints and usually letting it all cook on a low heat overnight before making the leap from notion to action.

(Foundation for People with Learning Disabilities, 1999)

Yet this opportunity is often restricted or denied to people with high support needs.
Paul Hocker concluded:

Everyone has the right to choose. It is part of the work to make society aware of this and accepting of this.

Choice is a right, an expression of self-determination, and to deny this is a form of oppression. We also live in a society where the market economy and consumer choice is paramount and people with high support needs should be able share in this. At the same time, we recognise that choices are not unlimited and, indeed, that unfettered choice can be bewildering.

This raises the issue of how valid it is to offer a range of choices, when life experiences are limited. It was important to explore ways of offering alternatives to participants in the projects that were meaningful and to ask whether wider options were confusing or whether they could lead to greater and welcome opportunities. We also needed to monitor how people expressed their wishes, from their individual perspective.

Some of the grant applications we received were focusing on enabling people to exercise choice within a narrow range of options. For example, one proposal focused on ways of presenting options for meals in a home. For the Choice Initiative this was too limited. We wanted projects which would tackle more complex issues, such as engaging in the community, making and sustaining friendships and participating in the world of work.

We decided we would need to monitor
- how participants expressed their wishes
- how choices were presented
- whether options appeared to be meaningful
- whether participants' communication developed, as choices were listened to
- how choices were supported
- the impact of choice on participants' lives
- the nature of obstacles to choice.

Project staff would record developments, but we would also seek the views of carers, key workers or employers about the impact of the Choice Initiative on the lives of participants. We would need to document negative experiences and identify barriers to choice.

We also needed to recognise that choice could be dangerous. Margaret Flynn (1999) has since shown how the over zealous support of choice has threatened people's health. The Foundation therefore funded Professor Andy Alaszewski to research agencies' policies on risk assessment and risk management, and to identify the principles and examples of good practice and procedures for adults with learning disabilities in the community (Alaszewzki et al, 1999).

Choice in context

Many agencies quote John O'Brien's Five Principles (O'Brien and Tyne, 1981) as the philosophy underpinning their services, including the importance of extending choice, but are they reflected in the reality of individual lives? Have service providers explored their meaning for people with high support needs?

In view of the limited research into issues of choice for people with high support needs, it was hoped that a programme of innovative service development projects would throw light on some of the key issues, such as the benefits of choice to the individual, whether learned helplessness is a factor, and the conditions under which choice can best be presented (Stalker and Harris, 1998).

It is also important to consider the issues linked to choice in the context of current social policy. Recent legislation and policies have created greater opportunities for choice to be expressed. The NHS and Community Care Act (1990) has paved the way for assessing and meeting individual need. It is important that people with high support needs can be listened to, so that their lives are not determined solely by other people.

The continuing debate about the role of day centres and the development of other options such as further education and employment are likely to expand choice. Recent government statements about social inclusion, employment and lifelong learning have reinforced this, but people with high support needs are in danger of being left behind.

We welcome the setting up of the Disability Rights Commission and the opportunities it will afford to strengthen the entitlement of people with learning disabilities to participate fully in the community.

This exploration of the lives of people with high support needs has also been particularly timely in the light of the government's current development of a national strategy for people with learning disabilities.

Throughout the Choice Initiative we recorded the obstacles and difficulties to challenge the social exclusion of many people with high support needs.

Choice also had to be considered within the context of changing staff roles. Michael Smull has identified three components of choice: preferences, opportunities and control. He suggests that staff will need to listen to what people are saying, try to find ways of responding if at all possible and seek to minimise their own control. "Control is not a fixed quantity. It ebbs and flows in our relationships and it can ebb and flow with people we support" (Smull, 1995). In releasing control, doors are opened, but there is also the duty to keep people safe and this may place limits on choice.

It is recognised that staff and volunteers will need to be trained and supported in their evolving role. There will be special issues concerning the unique role that advocacy can play in exercising choice.

The projects

The Foundation has worked closely with the five projects over two and a half years, monitoring and evaluating the findings, making visits, supporting project staff through a series of workshops and meetings, and disseminating preliminary findings and project news through a series of bulletins. We also held a major conference, *Communication Matters,* in March 1999.

Four of the five projects were based in service-providing voluntary organisations. The fifth was based within the British Institute of Learning Disabilities (BILD). The following brief description of individual projects sets out their aims and methodologies.

The Step Out Project, L'Arche, Liverpool

L'Arche is an international network of communities founded by Jean Vanier where people with learning disabilities and their 'assistants' live and work together. There are workshops within some of the communities, but in 1996, in response to some of its members asking to enter mainstream employment, L'Arche in Liverpool set up a Job Club for those who were interested and six people were found work placements.

Several people with high support needs were among those attending the Job Club and they too were asking for work in the community. An application was made to the Foundation to fund two part-time job trainers, who, together with the supported employment co-ordinator, would support four people with high support needs in each of two years, so that eventually an additional eight people would be receiving this service.

The aims included facilitating choice, promoting self-determination, supporting skills development and raising awareness of the availability of work for people with high support needs.

Eight people have been supported, six of whom have experienced work placements, and the supported employment scheme will continue. The findings are mainly discussed in Chapter 4.

The Friendship Train, People to People, London

With funding from the Foundation, People to People aimed to extend its existing work with people with mild learning disabilities. Two part-time facilitators worked with the agency's Director to encourage the development of friendships among young people with high support needs, to tackle loneliness and isolation, to raise awareness about friendship and to increase understanding about ways of facilitating choice. Paul Cambridge from the Tizard Centre has evaluated the Friendship Train.

The original plan was that, supported by a key person in their lives and the two facilitators, participants would meet together fortnightly, and hopefully, linking with others with whom they shared interests and demonstrated an affinity, would engage in social activity together.

The project was subsequently modified to link people in immediate neighbourhoods. The approach was further modified, with the facilitators moving into working through several group homes in order to provide a framework to facilitate friendship. The interesting and challenging findings from this project are described mainly in Chapter 5.

Choices Project, Markfield Project, London

The Markfield Project provides a range of activities for children and adults with learning disabilities and their families, including a weekly sensory session for those with high support needs. With funding from the Foundation, they were seeking to build on this. In a more flexible and individualised way, they sought to listen to participant's choices and to offer real opportunities to access the kind of mainstream community facilities which non-disabled people take for granted.

Eight people have been supported – on a ratio of two staff to one participant – to express their wishes and to engage in a variety of activities of their choice.

Choices has been managed by a part-time project worker assisted by paid sessional workers and volunteers. The valuable findings from this project are mainly discussed in Chapter 3.

The Futures Project, Choice Support, London

Originally based in the Southwark Brokerage Project until that agency was disbanded, the Futures Project aimed to work with young people with high support needs to develop choices about what they would do after leaving school. The aim was to discover and record their preferences with support from a part-time project worker. He was based in a local special school and worked with ten students.

The vehicle that was developed to capture the wishes and aspirations, as well as the descriptions of the young people's lives was a Communication Passport, which is described in Chapter 2. This has great potential, if used properly, to make the school-leaver's transition process smoother. The Communication Passport could also be used throughout the person's adult life.

Pathways to Citizen Advocacy, British Institute of Learning Disabilities (BILD)

The fifth project was rather different. In the belief that citizen advocacy has an important role to play in supporting choice, a part-time worker was funded to research, consult, write and pilot resource materials for use by local advocacy groups, entitled *Pathways to Citizen Advocacy* (BILD, 2000).

The Foundation Units cover key areas such as communication, choice and decision-making. The Advocacy in Context Units enable the partner to have a greater awareness of issues in the lives of people with severe learning disabilities, such as choice in where to live, daytime opportunities and the law. The project findings are described in Chapter 7, while material from the units has also been used in other chapters.

Capturing the learning?

These five projects have enabled us to reflect on a range of issues concerning choices for people with high support needs. Drawing on the rich and varied written and oral materials about the work, including the interim and final reports, the rest of this book seeks to capture the learning which everyone involved with the Choice Initiative has experienced. Material from the projects quoted verbatim usually appears in a purple panel.

Rather than reporting on a project-by-project basis, a series of chapters explores the issue of choice in various contexts. We have invited those with expertise in the areas covered by the Choice Initiative to write introductions to the chapters, so that the findings can be set in context.

Conclusion

One of the participants in the Step Out project was invited to take part in a workshop at a conference on supported employment. With the help of a video clip and overheads showing him at work in a motorbike showroom and car wash, Chris described his chosen placements with enthusiasm, words tumbling over one another. With his permission, Joe, his job trainer, explained further what Chris was saying.

The message from Chris and other people with learning disabilities who took part in the conference was that people were gaining control over their lives. The difference was that Chris needed greater support. A key message in this book is that people with high support needs can make choices in a meaningful way and can have control in their lives. It will look at how staff and volunteers can work effectively with them. But society too will need to change if people with high support needs are to be fully included and allowed to play a part in their communities as equal citizens.

Hazel Morgan

Hazel Morgan

Programme Manager, The Foundation for People with Learning Disabilities

Alaszewski, A., Alaszewki, H. and Parker, A. (1999) *Empowerment and Protection.* London: Mental Health Foundation.

British Institute of Learning Disabilities (2000) *Pathways to Citizen Advocacy.* Kiddermister: BILD.

Flynn, M., Fovargue, S. and Keywood, K. (1999) *Best Practice? Health Care Decision-Making By, With and For Adults with Learning Disabilities.* Manchester: The National Development Team.

Foundation for People with Learning Disabilities (1999) *The Choice Initiative: Bulletin No. 7 (Autumn 1999).* London: Foundation for People with Learning Disabilities.

Mental Health Foundation (1996a) *Building Expectations: Opportunities and Services for People with a Learning Disability.* London: Mental Health Foundation.

Mental Health Foundation (1996b) *Building Expectations: Inquiry into Opportunities and Services for People with Learning Disabilities.* London: Mental Health Foundation.

Mental Health Foundation (1997) *Building Expectations* video. London: Mental Health Foundation.

O'Brien, J. and Tyne, A. (1981) *The Principle of Normalisation: A Foundation for Effective Services.* London: Campaign for Mentally Handicapped People / Community and Mental Handicap Educational and Research Association.

Smull, M. (1995) *Revisiting Choice* in News and Notes. American Association for Mental Retardation.

Stalker, K. and Harris, P. (1998) *The Exercise of Choice by Adults with Intellectual Disabilities: A Literature Review.* Journal of Applied Research Intellectual Disabilities, Kidderminster: British Institute of Learning Disabilities 11, 1: 60-76.

Communication
and choice

INTRODUCTION

The importance of communication

Communication lies at the heart of our ability to function as fully participating members of society. Human beings have evolved an immensely subtle, dynamic and flexible communication system through which they are enabled to give and receive information. However, anyone who has tried to sort out a problem in a country where they don't have an adequate knowledge of the local language will have experienced the frustration and embarrassment of not understanding or being understood.

Society places a high value on the ability to use spoken and written language. Education depends on it. Relationships depend on it. Anyone who does not have adequate skills in the understanding and expression of their native language is likely to be devalued by society. The consequence is that they undervalue themselves and are socially 'disabled'.

The majority of people acquire communication skills through a developmental process, which begins at birth and continues to grow and develop throughout life. The acquisition of speech and language happens so apparently effortlessly that it is only when it does not happen, or when illness or trauma remove or damage it, that the devaluing effect can be fully recognised.

The very ease with which most people learn to communicate leads them to make major and often damaging assumptions about the process when working or meeting with those who cannot. In a sense, we all consider ourselves experts because we can do it.

Successful communication depends on having something to say, a way of saying it and someone to listen who shares the same *method* – in other words, a common language. Because spoken language is the method of communication favoured by society, there is real pressure on people to learn to speak.

There is also an assumption that someone who can say one word, must be able to say and *understand* many words. This is a natural human assumption: someone learns a few words of French before crossing the Channel, for example, but when they utter *"Bonjour"* and are met with a barrage of incomprehensible jargon, they are left feeling embarrassed, stupid and at a loss. Such feelings are experienced whenever communication breaks down and the frustration arising from prolonged inability to 'get a message across' can, and often does, lead to anger or withdrawal from the situation.

People with severe or profound learning disabilities (hereafter referred to as people with high support needs) have severe or profound difficulty with communicating through spoken language. They may have no recognisable means of expressing themselves and become frustrated through their inability to affect or control their lives through shared understanding. The frustration may be expressed in behaviour perceived as challenging or in withdrawal from human contact. The frustration is often shared by those who live and work with them and attempts to deal with the difficulties may lead to misunderstanding, tokenism, inappropriate use of alternative methods or avoidance of the problem.

Since communication is at one and the same time *uniquely individual and commonly shared,* any 'strategy' aimed at providing services for people with high support needs should reflect both facets if it is to succeed

From the medical to the social model

It is not that long since many people with high support needs were shut away in institutions and training centres, receiving little more than personal care. Expectations of progress were minimal or non-existent, and the idea that people could exercise any control over their own lives through learning new ways of doing so had not dawned. The medical model was deeply entrenched in the provision of care and the emphasis was on changing people with disabilities so that they conformed to society's view of 'normality' rather than changing society's view of 'normality'.

The influence of 'normalisation' (O'Brien and Tyne, 1981) on policy-makers and the ensuing move from institution-based to community care reduced segregation, but there was – and often continues to be – a 'black hole' in the knowledge, skills and resources available to staff and carers attempting to support people in their new environment. The move towards a social model of disability which requires others to make reasonable adjustments affects communication more than any other aspect of human behaviour. Inclusion is not only about ramps and lifts!

Over the last two decades, great efforts have been made to fill the 'black hole'. However, the need to fulfil the aspirations of policy-makers, together with limited available resources and interventions have often led to an unintentional 'tokenism'. Increasing recognition of the value of alternative ways of communicating has opened up new possibilities for many individuals, but has often led to professionals and carers frantically searching for solutions and 'packages', which may or may not be appropriately applied and which are used in a fragmentary fashion.

Since all individuals are, by definition, different, communication 'tools' have to be tailored to individual need. This presents a major difficulty. As mentioned above, communication only works if it is commonly understood. Most human beings acquire a commonly understood native language early in their lives. Asking this majority to learn *other* ways of communicating, in order to accommodate and include the minority who have not acquired this common language, may be unachievable. What we may be able to do, though, is bring together and share all our current experience and knowledge so we can attempt to build a common approach across services systems and organisational boundaries.

The communication needs of people with learning disabilities encompass the whole developmental range. From those who have reasonable understanding and use of spoken language, but who may have limited or non-existent literacy skills, through those who can use formal and more standardised alternatives such as signing and symbols, through those who may use less formal and more concrete forms of communication such as photographs and objects of reference, to those who have no immediately and commonly recognisable form of communication and who depend on the interpretation of their communication behaviour by other people.

The development of communication allows people to move from being reactive to being pro-active. Nowhere is this more evident than in the matter of choice. This book is primarily concerned with people whose lack of language makes it hard for them to be pro-active and experience the joy of interacting with others.

Many people in this group have missed out on the basic building blocks of communication and sociability. The development of sociability and communication starts with the mother-infant interaction – gazing at one another, both maybe babbling or making 'noises' and moving on to speech. With the child with severe learning disabilities, this natural interaction may be distorted or absent: eye contact may be difficult, or there may be a lack of responsiveness. As they grow older, they may continue to be denied such interactions through the insistence on (chronological) age-appropriateness applied by politically correct agencies/departments.

Intensive Interaction

The complexity and importance of early interactions in developing the basics of communication with people with high support needs has been extensively researched by Nind and Hewett (1994). Their practical and accessible 'Intensive Interaction' approach is designed to assist the development of communication and sociability, based on the idea that fundamental abilities are "learned in the first year of life without being consciously taught". Nind and Hewett have shown that "interactive play has a crucial role in ongoing development. The approach involves the participants in the kind of learning experiences and processes through which sociability and communication develop in infancy. It is the process rather than the outcome of the sequences that is central to the method." The 'naturalness' of this approach means that many carers/staff already intuitively possess the skills and abilities to put it into practice, though they may need reassurance that it is acceptable to do so.

Nind and Hewett define Intensive Interaction as

> an approach which is relevant for people who may be pre-verbal, not at a stage of understanding verbal or symbolic communication. It may also be relevant for the people we meet who have some spoken language but who do not use it to communicate. Their speech may be accompanied by a sense of remoteness and lack of any facial expression, eye contact, or pauses for the other person's turn. It is for people who have few or limited communication behaviours and who lack the skills needed for being social with other people. Intensive Interaction is about reaching those learners who do not yet know that being with another human being can be pleasurable or can be under their control. Their general tempo of living may be very different and they may be withdrawn. It is for those people whose signals we do not understand and whom we may have some difficulty in perceiving as being social and communicative.
> *(1994: 13)*

Developing a more coherent approach

There is a growing interest in the use of Intensive Interaction and interactive approaches around the UK. It has been introduced, as with many of the other approaches to communication, by a range of practitioners in different settings. Most speech and language therapists working in this field have some knowledge and/or awareness of the approach. Many teachers, psychologists, staff, carers and others across the whole range of agencies and service provision around the country are at different stages of embracing interactive approaches.

The philosophical approach, which puts the individual at the centre and starts 'where the person is', allows that individual to interact at whichever level and by whichever method of communication they are able. The earlier this is in the developmental continuum, the less formal and standardised it will be. The onus will be on the other person to learn to know, interpret, understand and respond. As people progress towards more symbolic ways of communicating, the use of objects or photographs may be introduced. These are likely to be very personal and based on the daily needs and choices of the individual.

When the use of signing and symbols is introduced, the question of standardisation raises its head. It clearly makes sense to attempt some level of consensus especially when there is an ever-increasing demand for official documents and information in general to be accessible to everyone. However, there are currently different systems in use across the UK with many local variations. The language of signs and symbols needs to reflect spoken and written language in allowing generation at personal and local level, but we also need a national 'thesaurus' available to all.

New ways of working with communication are still being introduced in an inconsistent fashion, depending largely on individual practitioner's beliefs, training, influence and experience and the agency they happen to be working for. While some practitioners have already assimilated these new approaches and have radically influenced service provision and the quality of life for people with high support needs, many others have not even heard of them.

Provision of speech therapy is also patchy: one county, for example, has one speech and language therapist for all adults with learning disabilities, whilst a neighbouring county has seven for a similar population.

There is no agreed common body of knowledge, skills and attitudes for professionals working in this field. There is no cohesive approach to developing a common strategy for individual communication and no agreed skill mix of professionals in disability services. Speech and language therapists have no consensus about the approaches they promote.

There is still considerable debate around health/social care/education issues. People are caught up in a constantly shifting philosophical and political scene. With such a fragmented and arbitrary situation, people will continue to try to do whatever they can within their own sphere of influence. The inevitable result is lack of cohesion, re-invention of the wheel and a proliferation of different 'systems' and 'packages' adding to the confusion.

Communication and inclusion

The implications for society in developing social inclusion are many. The fundamental nature of communication in the process is clear. Society needs to widen its understanding and acceptance of all forms of communication which will require a comprehensive and continuing learning process for all, starting with those who are nearest to people with high support needs and moving out with them into wider society. Before this can happen, there needs to be a national initiative to address the current confusion and to create a cohesive approach. There is no choice without a voice.

The American Speech and Hearing Association issued a Communication Bill of Rights in 1992 through the National Joint Committee for the Communication Needs of Persons with Severe Disabilities. It is reproduced here with their permission.

A COMMUNICATION BILL OF RIGHTS

All persons, regardless of the extent or severity of their disabilities, have a basic human right to affect through communication the conditions of their own existence. Beyond the general right, a number of specific communication rights should be ensured in all daily interactions involving persons who have severe disabilities. These basic communication rights are as follows.

1. The right to request desired objects, actions, events and persons and to express personal preferences or feelings.

2. The right to be offered choices and alternatives.

3. The right to reject or refuse undesired objects, events or actions including the right to decline or reject all proferred choices.

4. The right to request and be given attention from and interaction with another person.

5. The right to request feedback or information about a state, an object, a person or an event of interest.

6. The right to active treatment and intervention efforts to enable people with severe disabilities to communicate messages in whatever modes and as effectively and efficiently as their specific abilities will allow.

7. The right to have communicative acts acknowledged and responded to, even when the intent of these acts cannot be fulfilled by the responder.

8. The right to have access at all times to any needed augmentative and alternative communication devices and other assistive devices and to have those devices in good working order.

9. The right to environmental contexts, interactions and opportunities that expect and encourage persons with disabilities to participate as full communicative partners with other people including peers.

10. The right to be informed about people, things and events in one's immediate environment.

11. The right to be communicated with in a manner that recognises and acknowledges the inherent dignity of the person being addressed including the right to be part of communication exchanges about the individual that are conducted in his or her presence.

12. The right to be communicated with in ways that are meaningful, understandable and culturally and linguistically appropriate.

Herb Lovett, in his book *Learning to Listen* (1996) makes the following observation:

> If we really want a society for us all, we need to turn the questions from "What is wrong with you so that you can't be a full member of society?" to ask instead "How have we collectively built a society that keeps you out?" "What do you have to bring?" "What has your life taught you and what can we learn from you?" *(1996: 7)*

No liberation movement has ever required the people who are excluded to change. After a generation of struggle, the most recent wave of liberation movements – of women, African Americans, Latinos and homosexuals – have all made some small progress, but women did not become men, African Americans did not become white and Latinos did not abandon their culture nor homosexuals their sexuality. Progress has come from changes in the exclusionist attitudes of the mainstream culture. In this context – and the context of a liberation movement is critical to this point – it makes sense that, instead of trying to make people with learning disabilities act and appear 'more normal', our energies would be best spent in learning to respect the existing skills of people and the choices they have already made as our first step towards a fully inclusive society.

Jane Jones

Jane Jones

Chief Executive, Somerset Total Communication

The Projects' Experience
communication and choice

Without exception, all the Choice Initiative projects found that establishing a means of communication was an essential starting-point before issues of choice could begin to be addressed. Moreover, as Jane Jones' introduction to this chapter makes clear, communication develops within the context of relationships, starting in the first year of life.

> The foundation of this work has been to find ways of building relationships and communication skills, which enable us to determine, establish and fulfil individual needs.

Building relationships

Providing opportunities for the person with high support needs and the project worker to develop a relationship was one of the most time-consuming aspects of the work, but a necessary building-block which often took considerably longer than the projects had anticipated at the planning stage.

While some participants already had people in their lives with whom they communicated in some fashion, others were very isolated. It was important to be sensitive to this and not force people to interact until they were ready to do so, otherwise they could well feel invaded, imposed on or overwhelmed. Many participants were very used to being part of groups where opportunities to learn how to build one-to-one relationships were limited or non-existent.

> Andreas, a young man living in a small group home, was someone who seemed to resist contact with other people. Although he would occasionally smile, he mostly growled or pushed people away and certainly did not like to be touched. Staff in the home found his resistance to eye contact, physical contact and interaction as much of a challenge as any violent behaviour would have been.

> The staff member of the Futures Project who was working with a group of young people in a special school soon realised that he needed to spend time which "allowed for mutual understanding and familiarity to develop... and for each person to adjust to having a stranger in their midst." Working on individual portfolios meant asking personal questions and this could not start until everyone had got to know and trust one another.

In Step Out, the project manager already knew the people they were working with, although the project workers were newly recruited. At Markfield, although some participants were known to the project, the Choices staff and volunteers still had to get to know the individual people they were working with. Knowing something about an individual was helpful, but the one-to-one relationship building was still an important stage in the project work.

BILD's advocacy project also prioritised the advocacy partnership and the need to focus on building a relationship and establishing two-way communication from the start. The training materials which were produced covered key topics around communication, with a particular emphasis on establishing communication with people who have high support needs and do not communicate verbally.

Building trust and self-confidence

The relationships needed to allow both parties to develop trust, belief and confidence in one another. Moving on to making choices and trying out new experiences was often frightening for participants. These fears were to some extent inevitable, but people needed to feel safe enough to risk change.

Step Out saw that people needed time to build trust before they felt ready to take the leap into work; they needed opportunities to share fears and expectations and know that they were being supported. This can be a difficult and stressful experience for both parties, particularly in the early days.

> It was hard work being with Andrew. I had no trust in him and he had no trust in me. I remember going with him to the volunteer bureau to see if he could experience lots of different work tasters to see what would interest him. Andrew would not walk. He refused to put one foot in front of the other. We were late for the interview and when we got there, Andrew spent the whole time saying he felt sick. He was clearly unsure about the whole thing and we had to take time in our relationship, allowing him to make choices and me to listen and understand him.

An important element in the relationships was helping people to develop self-confidence and a belief in their abilities. People with high support needs are often viewed as unskilled and unable. Challenging those beliefs was essential. Project workers needed to believe in the person's potential before that person could start to believe in themselves.

Allowing time for relationships to develop

All the projects were working with people on a part-time basis and while this probably meant that relationships took longer to develop, it also became clear that forcing the pace – perhaps by spending more time with individuals each week – would not necessarily have been the best way forward.

> Despite their growing relationship, Andreas has also shown his own need for space... being focused on can be very intense.

Adopting a pace which people can manage may sometimes be difficult, particularly where there is an emphasis on 'outcomes', 'results' or 'numbers'. The Foundation's recognition of the importance of this issue enabled staff to work at each person's individual pace.

> In getting to know Paul, I realise the importance of taking time... I am also learning the wisdom of not rushing into things, to go gently with humility and respect.

Contexts for relationship building

Getting to know one another often seemed to work best when project staff spent time in the individual's own territory – generally this was where they lived, but could also be in day service settings.

Step Out's supported employment workers were part of the existing L'Arche community and were able to become directly involved in people's daily routines without too much difficulty. Both workers were able to tap into the life of the community, sharing meals in people's houses, joining in their parties, going on holiday with them and sharing activities in the community such as shopping or swimming. The workers also spent time with some people in the L'Arche workshops, which also enabled them, to see people in a work setting.

> Paul's job trainer found a number of ways of enabling them to get to know each other; he began by spending time with Paul when he was with people he already knew and trusted; he shared in some of Paul's existing routines such as going to the library on Wednesday afternoons; he also joined in social events where Paul was present. Alongside this he was learning to communicate with Paul and discovering how Paul could communicate with him.

Sometimes projects found they needed to try out different ways of beginning to build a relationship. Some people needed the routine of meeting at a regular time on the same day each week and perhaps in the same setting; this structure provided a sense of security, enabling people to start out on the risky business of interacting with other people.

A two-way process

Although this chapter has largely focused on the need for project workers to get to know participants, relationship building is a two-way process. The person being supported needs to get to know their project worker.

The Futures Project worker devised his own way of enabling the school students to get to know him. He made a series of short videos about his home life, his friends, his pets, his favourite pubs and local places that were important to him. This also modelled important elements of relationships, including sharing information about oneself with others and having tastes and preferences of one's own.

> I found that this brought an early acceptance and understanding of individual taste and opinion, which was a vital ingredient in our later attempts at making personal statements to form a Communication Passport. I was seeking to find the individual in each of them by allowing them to share aspects of my individuality.

Learning from other people

All the projects found it helpful at times to seek the views of other people, particularly in the early stages when they were getting to know a person and when those who were close to them could contribute to the process.

Meeting someone for the first time, it can be difficult (or even impossible) to understand the meaning of their communication. As the Friendship Train's staff discovered, asking the carer to interpret someone's facial gestures, movements or shouts at the first meeting was often invaluable in helping to ascertain whether the person might be interested in participating in the project. Carers can also suggest possible activities and interests.

> Simon's mum was able to tell the sessional worker that he enjoyed football and this became a starting-point for their activities together.

Step Out project workers spent time with participants in different settings. This helped them get to know people in a familiar setting but also meant they could draw on other people's knowledge and experience.

> Spending time with Diane in the Therapy Project and working together in the L'Arche shop was not only a good starting-point but also allowed me to learn from others who already knew Diane.

> Joining in with Alan's routine, participating in his day care schedule such as going bowling, enabled me to learn from people Alan already trusted.

Communication with families and others

All the projects were involved with participants on a part-time basis and it was important to develop good collaborative relationships with families and care staff.

Finding out what someone's life has been like and getting a picture of their past could be helpful when trying to understand the person as they are now.

> Establishing satisfactory communication has been difficult with Sandra, who, as well as having a severe learning disability, has a hearing impairment and cataracts in both eyes. This can be frustrating for her and other people, but finding out more about her past, which included spending two-thirds of her life in a long-stay hospital, has helped the project understand more about Sandra's difficulties.

Involving other people also provided opportunities for challenging existing expectations about a person such as "X will never cope with that" or "Y will never be able to go out to work". People with high support needs often acquire negative or stigmatising labels during their lives which can inhibit other people from seeing them in a more positive light.

Where projects were working with individuals from minority ethnic communities, communication with families could also present difficulties, as the Futures Project found. In some cases, English was the second or even third language within the family. In the case of a Greek Cypriot participant, for example, although the family seemed happy that their son was involved in the project, the worker was uncertain how much they actually understood about the Communication Passport and generally what was involved.

In some instances, cultural norms may have led the family to acquiesce with the project's aims and the reasons for it, but when the project worker talked with professionals afterwards, it emerged that key family members had not really understood the discussions or what it was they had agreed to.

Lack of clear communication could have a significant knock-on effect as relatives often act as role models. If key family members are not committed to the project's aims, or do not understand the reasons for it, the individual will not feel supported by family members and may only participate in a token fashion. It would almost certainly have been helpful if interpreters had been involved with some families.

Understanding non-verbal communication

People whose use of speech is limited or non-existent nevertheless have many different ways of 'speaking'. The challenge for others is to reach a shared understanding of what an individual wants to communicate – boredom, pleasure, or whatever. Although some participants in the Choice Initiative used Makaton, signing or facilitating communication, this was by no means universal and was never the only means of communication individuals used; each person had unique and individual ways of communicating.

> Amy communicated using a variety of strong facial expressions, different vocalisations, body language, whole body action and by taking things or people she wants. When happy, she would giggle or grin with open body language; when in distress, she would grimace, throw her head back, stand up and make hooting noises. More subtle expressions would communicate her need for food, drink or to go to the toilet.

> Darren uses a gurgling sound and eye contact to communicate. He has a particular skill in communicating, using his eyelids to respond to questions from others; usually a 'yes' or 'no' can be deciphered from this method.

Understanding 'communication' means not just recognising that a person is communicating but also understanding its meaning. This can be particularly relevant when thinking about someone's behaviour. 'Challenging behaviour' is still too often seen as a problem which must be managed, rather than as a communicative act needing to be interpreted and understood. Someone who repeatedly runs to the door of the pub and growls, for example, may simply be 'saying': "I don't want to be in this place because it's too noisy and smoky" or "I've spent enough time here, let's go and do something else". Too often, though, the response is to try and get the person to remain in the situation, even if they are finding it distressing, unpleasant or just plain boring. Project workers needed to be aware of the kinds of things to watch and listen for when with an individual and what the range of communication encompasses.

> First there is a need for workers to actively listen to sounds, words, scratches or tapping, but also to listen for silences and consider what sounds interest the participant. People with visual impairment have shown this to be more important for their involvement. There is a need to watch for eye contact, facial expression, physical expression or behaviours. Tracking for eye contact is not just about noting every time someone looks into the other person's eyes but a more general awareness – where the eyes usually look, changes in the quality of the look – towards or away – where the person's interest is at any one time and when that interest is lost. We can then confirm and develop that interest or response – or vice versa.

One project recorded the many different ways in which participants used to communicate without using words, which included the following:

- eye contact • where people look • what people look at • blinking
- raising an eyebrow • listening • facial expressions • sighing • shouting • crying
- laughing • humming • growling • moving closer to someone • moving away
- tense or relaxed body • pointing and gesturing • reaching for something
- pushing someone or something away • tapping • general restlessness.

This list is not exhaustive but hopefully conveys something of the very wide range of ways in which people may communicate and the importance of closely attending to the other person.

Individual communication

Learning about an individual's means of communicating was an integral part of developing a communication partnership.

> An individualised approach was essential for people with high support needs. In practice much depended on informal and unstructured systems of communication – verbal and non-verbal cues, voice tone, body language, facial expression, eye contact and so on.

For some people, it was important to allow enough time for them to consider what they wanted to communicate, maybe to evaluate various options, before responding.

> Susan needs time to speak and answer questions, sometimes she needs 15 seconds or longer... she knows what she likes and will make a yes or no answer to questions, sometimes she will debate questions with herself, but she always needs plenty of time and she is not a person to be rushed.

The way a person expresses themselves can be very subtle. In the Friendship Train, for example, one participant who did not use speech and was blind expressed his likes and dislikes in quite complex ways:

> One of the ways in which he might express not liking something is to hit people... reach out and give people a smack... and it's important for the people working with him to see the difference between what might be a very hard smack and a gentle push which might mean something very different.

Developing ways of communicating

As Jane Jones suggested in her introduction to this chapter, the key to unlocking communicating is often seen to lie in finding the right package or set of tools, which can be applied to anyone.

> I think I had this fantasy that there was going to be a load of tools that we would be able to use... and that we'd be able to use them to create friendships.

From the experience of the Choice Initiative projects, it is evident that communication is highly individual and cannot be developed with off-the-shelf packages or approaches. They did discover, though, there *are* tools and techniques, though they may not appear immediately obvious. Often they are:

> very basic simple things like paying close attention to people, not making assumptions about people, really listening and realising that even when people are quiet they are perhaps communicating; and some people have very subtle and complex ways of expressing themselves.

With some participants, it was possible to tap into and use existing communication tools while with others these were introduced if it seemed appropriate. These included:

Using objects of reference *Sandra's worker uses Sandra's bag and her own car keys to indicate that this is going to be a Choices session.*

Mirroring *Tina expresses happiness by skipping; her support workers validate this by joining in and being part of her happiness.*

Use of pictures *The Friendship Train facilitators used pictures of different social activities, when making initial visits to potential participants.*

Sometimes the project workers had to try out different ways of communicating with people. Music was used to build a rapport with some of the students in the Futures Project. Paul's supported employment worker facilitated him to type out his feelings about work. All the projects used photographs in different contexts.

Choosing how to communicate

Choice can start with learning about the ways a person wants to communicate and supporting their choice – which might include allowing that person *not* to communicate on some occasions. Projects sometimes found that although an individual had been taught to use a particular communication method, such as signing or facilitated communication, they were refusing to use it or doing so very reluctantly.

> Lewis had been assessed by speech therapists and taught lip reading and Makaton, but the project worker found he often resisted using them.

> Diane is capable of using facilitated communication; however, she does not always choose to communicate in this way and will express this by banging her head and screaming.

A particular communication method should not be imposed on anyone who seems very resistant, as they will almost certainly refuse to use it – though it is important to try and ascertain possible reasons why this is happening. Interaction has to be enjoyable otherwise withdrawal is likely to ensue. For example, if someone clearly dislikes and resists being touched, they will not respond well to any attempts to use physical contact.

Recording and remembering ways of communicating

Communication between two individuals is a particular and often unique experience, so all the projects found they needed to develop ways of recording and remembering what each participant 'said', and how and what they communicated. This had a number of benefits:

- a tangible way for individuals to 'own' information about themselves
- a way of sharing information with others
- it could help staff and carers communicate with and support people in a more consistent fashion
- new staff could use the information to get to know the person (although it should never be used as a substitute for getting to know someone directly)
- ensuring that important information about a person does not get lost.

Each project found different ways of recording information, including Communication Passports, portfolios, photo albums and feedback forms.

The Communication Passport

The Futures Project's main aim was to help a group of young people to produce individual Communication Passports.

> A special way of recording what you want to say about yourself, using eye-catching layout and imagery. It gives you the voice that is often unheard, from humour to anger, and may invite others to add their positive comments too. It lets staff know you as you wish to be known and treated. It lets your style of communication receive recognition and it can also grow into a unique record of personal development.

A Communication Passport should be
- personal
- have a simple, clear and accessible layout
- easy to manage
- visually attractive
- robust
- interactive
- open-ended, allowing for new entries
- graphical.

Each Communication Passport is individually tailored but may include
- an introduction
- rules of use
- communication (you and me)
- likes and dislikes
- feelings
- relationships
- abilities
- achievements
- aims

- styles of learning
- health
- training and employment
- other information
- acknowledgements.

Although the Communication Passport can be a very powerful tool, it should perhaps also carry a 'use with care' warning with the following information:

- work should not start on the Communication Passport until a relationship of trust has been established between the individual and whoever is supporting them to produce the Passport
- the person should *always* be at the centre of the process of developing the Communication Passport
- the person should be supported in ways which ensure that they remain in control of the process at all times
- the Communication Passport should never be used by staff or anyone else as a substitute for spending time getting to know a person and developing a relationship with them
- the Communication Passport is *not* a care assessment or report
- ownership of the Communication Passport must remain with the individual and should never be shown to other people without their permission.

Making sure that someone really does have ownership of their Passport is not always straightforward and may require creative thinking and a conscious commitment to doing this. Service systems operate with files, notes and reports about individuals and, despite greater openness generally about records, the prevailing culture may not easily shift towards people owning what is written about them – especially if they have high support needs.

Portfolios and monitoring forms

The Step Out project found that building individual portfolios of the places people had visited and work they had done enabled them to share their experiences with peers, friends and other people.

An unforeseen development was that portfolios also enabled people to communicate more widely about being on the project as they empowered and enabled people to 'talk' in large groups, at conferences and in schools. At the launch party for the Foundation for People with Learning Disabilities in 1998, Alan, supported by his worker, Anna, described his work at the Toy Library. He did this using photographs projected onto a screen, with an audio-tape illustrating sounds at his workplace such as the telephone ringing and the washing machine whirring.

Markfield's Choices project recorded information about the participants through weekly feedback forms, which not only recorded the activities of that session but also had information about communication and choice making. This provided a constantly changing and evolving picture of someone and could be usefully shared with others.

> The lessons learned about Tina over the first year have been of great use to her new staff; having accurate feedback from project staff about just one like or dislike could facilitate the building of new relationships.

How people developed communication

A particularly rewarding feature of the Choice Initiative was the way in which individual participants began to open up to other people and communicate more freely. This could also be seen as validating the often time-consuming early stages when project workers were building relationships with individuals.

As project staff became familiar with individual participants, they were able to recognise changes in people's routine behaviour and responses. As the vignettes below illustrate, being able to communicate had a real 'ripple' effect. People became more confident and assertive, had better relationships and often enjoyed life a lot more.

> When Andrew joined Step Out he found it difficult to understand what other people were saying or communicate verbally himself. He tended to say "yes" when asked a question and would repeat phrases. Now Andrew chooses to communicate more and he gives people more eye contact, perhaps because he feels more self-confident.

> Alan uses speech, gesture and sound to communicate, but when he joined the project he generally talked in monosyllables and other people found his speech hard to understand. After 18 months, he continues to communicate both verbally and non-verbally, but he is much more confident about speaking, something which his supported employment worker has encouraged by getting him to use the telephone more.

> When Susan joined Step Out she was very withdrawn. She would curl up in a ball, hide her face and avoid eye contact. Although she could speak as well as sign, her verbal communication was limited to utterances such as "you picking on me" or "stop shouting at me". Since becoming a Step Out participant, Susan's communication with other people has changed considerably and she has blossomed. Her body language, eye contact and verbal communication have all flourished. Although she still needs encouragement to speak, she joins in conversations more readily, her voice is louder and her speech is clearer.

Using communication to make choices

By building relationships and establishing communication, people's likes and dislikes could begin to be expressed.

> Diane's Step Out worker felt that going into the community with her would not only help build their relationship but would also provide opportunities for Diane to make new choices. Diane has been very positive about going out and uses facilitated communication to express her choices. If Diane expresses an interest in going on the Mersey ferry, for example, she is given more information: how long the journey lasts, what times it leaves, the fact that she won't be able to get off it once they are on board. Diane then uses facilitated communication to tell her worker what she has chosen.

Conclusion

Communication and relationships are inextricably linked. Building a communication partnership between the project worker and the participant was the starting-point in enabling people to communicate and make choices. Without this it would have been difficult to have made progress. Like all relationships, this took time, time for people to feel secure, time for the project staff to learn a person's very individual and sometimes very subtle ways of communicating.

> The two people supporting Andreas in the community used his prompts about whether he wanted to walk, sit down somewhere or be pushed in his wheelchair as the starting-point for acting on his choices. Doing this regularly helped build a relationship where Andreas could give a signal and have it acted on – for example, rocking his chair forward to signal that he wanted to move on somewhere else. Andreas also began to take G's or S's hand when he wanted support or wanted to lead them somewhere.

Sometimes the changes in the life of the participant were very striking.

> When project staff first went to meet Tina, she mainly communicated by moaning, hitting herself and pacing up and down the room. After three months of weekly Choices sessions, Tina was no longer crying; she was laughing, singing and full of mischief. As the project worker observed: "she is a totally different person, full of character and fun".

Building relationships and communication were the doors to new opportunities. The Foundation for People with Learning Disabilities recorded how communication partnerships worked in three of the projects on a video. It is a resource in a training pack, *Choice Discovered*, for frontline workers.

O'Brien, J. and Tyne, A. (1981) *The Principle of Normalisation: A Foundation for Effective Services.* London: Campaign for Mentally Handicapped People (CMH) and Community and Mental Handicap Educational and Research Association (CMHERA).

Nind, M. and Hewett, D. (1994) *Access to Communication: Developing the Basics of Communication with People with Severe Learning Difficulties through Intensive Interaction.* London: David Fulton.

Lovett, H. (1996) *Learning to Listen: Positive Approaches and People with Difficult Behaviour.* London: Jessica Kingsley.

Mental Health Media (2000) *Choice Discovered.* London: Mental Health Media.

Choosing
community activities

INTRODUCTION

Many people with high support needs have dull daily routines, few relationships and little or no involvement in the local community. Achieving a better quality of life may be further hampered by limited support to communicate, having poor health care and few opportunities to influence the way in which funding for support is allocated. The Choice Initiative, however, has begun to address some of these issues.

This introduction looks at some recent developments which enable people to make real choices and be involved in their community.

People with high support needs often spend time in services which have remained largely unchanged for 20 years. The health and social care systems, which replaced long-stay hospitals, were designed to offer a safe environment which could meet people's 'special' needs. As a result, many people with high support needs have continued to experience considerable social isolation and low expectations about having a place in the community.

At the same time, there has been a growing recognition that we need to redesign services so that people with high support needs can be actively involved in choosing how they live. We now have a considerable body of knowledge about how to support people in their chosen lifestyle. We now need to use this knowledge to help individuals, step by step, to achieve their potential and carve out ways of participating in and contributing to life in the community. The real challenge lies in implementing values and beliefs, and in putting policies into practice.

New ways of seeing the world

The 1990s has been a decade of change in government thinking about community care. Policy statements have increasingly emphasised the desirability of community involvement, employment and a move away from segregated services. The importance of individual choice and control have been recurring themes. Demands for change have been made with varying degrees of intensity and there has been some limited progress in meeting these goals.

The long-stay hospital closure programme has been successful in terms of moving significant numbers of people out of institutions. Some of the resources formerly tied up in hospitals were reinvested in day centres. Relatively efficient planning processes of the early 1970s involved almost every community in the UK building or providing a day centre. As a result, most people with high support needs are still dependent on day centres for their day-to-day activities. Even within day centres, people needing significant levels of support are often confined to 'special care units', effectively placing them in double segregation and making their journey to community inclusion even more difficult.

Building-based support may seem more secure to family carers needing day-time respite and any change which threatens this important source of support may be difficult to implement.

Successful change will depend on changing the ways in which staff, carers and ordinary citizens perceive people with high support needs. The message needs to be clear: that with the right kind of individualised support, people who have been excluded, can be included and can make a contribution.

People's changing expectations

The lives of many young people with high support needs are very different from those of previous generations. The majority now remain at home where they and their families may be offered help in a variety of ways such as respite care or play schemes, for example. Whether they attend a special school or are supported in mainstream provision, parents and young people who have had a positive experience of support in the early years will expect adult services to enable the young person to participate in mainstream community activities such as college or work.

Services are beginning to emerge which support 19 year-olds to move from school to college and from college to finding a job. Adult education is offering more opportunities for young people leaving school, although it can be difficult for people to secure real paid employment. We are beginning to see a move away from the protective paternalism of services of the past towards measured risk-taking and supporting individuals to make choices.

The recent government document, *Learning to Succeed* (DfEE, 1999), recommends increasing educational opportunities for people with high support needs. The emphasis is on lifelong learning and the provision of inclusive education settings. Improved funding arrangements and more substantial support for people with high support needs are proposed. This should help to rectify the current situation where most people with high support needs have little or no access to post-school education.

A new national Learning and Skills Council, working with local learning and skills councils, will be responsible for strategic development, planning, funding management and quality assurance in all post-16 education. Under a common funding framework, all learners will be entitled to additional support and will resolve the current barriers to accessing funding where students are unable to meet the progression criteria.

There will be a new division focusing on provision for 16-19 years old and for over-19s. Young people will be supported by advisers, whose main role will be to guide and support individuals from the age of 13, helping to raise aspirations and addressing problems which may be hindering their progress.

These developments in post-school provision should make a significant contribution to improving the lifestyle choices of people with high support needs. However, it should be seen as one of a range of opportunities, alongside leisure, relationships, volunteering and employment opportunities, which can offer alternatives to traditional day centre provision.

The Choice Initiative did not receive any funding applications for projects specifically concerned with adult education, although the Futures Project was working with students in a special school, helping them to develop ways of making real choices about their post-school activities.

Having a job or undertaking work experience can be a powerful means of enabling people to participate in community life and Chapter 4 focuses on this, describing the experiences of Step Out in Liverpool.

Person-centred planning

The growth of person-centred planning has been one of the most significant changes in the last few years. If people's lives are to improve, then plans and goals need to be based on and built around their wishes, hopes and aspirations. The Changing Days project (McIntosh and Whittaker, 1998) sees this kind of planning as a key tool in developing individualised supports. It is based on the belief that people should have a regular opportunity to consider what they want in their lives, and be fully involved in decision-making about how they wish to be supported.

Person-centred planning seeks to ascertain what people want to do, how they want to live their lives, and then decides what needs to be done to make this happen. It emphasises taking action so that individuals' lives really change in measurable ways.

Person-centred planning needs to be a continuing process. The individual needs regular opportunities to meet with those involved in helping them plan. Goals, particularly early on, need to be achievable so that success can be celebrated and the person can move on to new horizons, with new goals.

The focus upon each person as a unique individual is particularly important for the person with high support needs. People who do not communicate verbally are more at risk of not being heard or simply not understood. Person-centred planning maximises a person's opportunities to influence decisions, empowers them and places them in the driving seat. The power is shifted so that people become the catalysts and designers of how support is offered.

A good person-centred plan will include consideration of the following questions:
- How do I communicate, particularly if I don't use words?
- What have I done so far in my life and what has my life been like?
- Who are the people in my life?
- What do I do now, where I do it, and who supports me?
- What say do I have in making decisions in my life?
- What are my abilities, talents and interests?
- What do I enjoy and what I do not enjoy?
- What do I want to do in the future?
- What support do I require?
- Who would I like to support me and in what way?
- What are the goals I have set for the next month, three months and year?
- What means and ways will be used to monitor progress that has been made on my goals?
- What are my health care needs and how can they be improved?

Staff who are involved in person-centred planning need certain skills and qualities which in many ways resemble those required from staff working in the Choice Initiative projects including the ability to engage with people who are non-verbal; being aware of, and able to react to, non-verbal communication; and enabling people to make their own decisions.

Person-centred planning and service development

Person-centred planning specifies clear outcomes. A meeting to plan for an individual should finish with clear goals and targets, clarity on what support is needed to reach these goals and who will provide this. More managers are now using the aggregation of these goals to map out future services. An example of this is in a day service where 80 people were involved in developing a person-centred plan for their future. Most people using the day centre had some complex disability. An analysis of the plans showed that about 30 per cent of people with complex disability wanted jobs, a high number of people wanted to be involved in local college courses, and another group wished to participate in the performing or visual arts. Moving from a service-led to a user-led approach to planning meant that day services could be redesigned in ways that were responsive to people's interests, hopes and expectations.

In the London Borough of Hackney, the *Me and My Community Initiative* (McIntosh and Whittaker, 2000) supported users in mapping out the resources and accessibility of a range of local community activities. Full-time staff supported individuals to do this, and find out more about the choices available as an alternative to the day service.

Another way of helping people with high support needs acquire a better quality of life is to plan day opportunities starting from where the person lives. In Cambridgeshire, a day opportunities worker helped people map out their individual preferred activities. Individuals were then supported to participate in a range of community-based activities, using their homes as the starting point and thus avoiding the need to travel to a day centre in order to go out. Starting from home helps people achieve ordinary patterns of living, without needing to use segregated settings as a stepping stone. The Hackney Community Resource Service is a non-buildings-based service which helps people with complex needs decide what they wish to do in the community, and supports them on a one-to-one basis. Most people spend two (and sometimes three) days a week participating in activities of their choice.

Changing roles for staff

The 1993 Community Care Act established a clear framework for care management. The expectation was that care managers would be accountable for the delivery and quality of individually designed care packages. In the event, many people with high support needs have not had those needs assessed within Social Services and do not receive a care package. In practice, frontline staff in residential and day services are often the main contributors to assessing the person's needs and supporting them to achieve their goals.

Increased opportunities for community involvement for people with high support needs have resulted in the development of a range of new job opportunities for staff, including job coaches in supported employment, leisure link workers, community bridge builders, community development workers and small business development workers. Alongside these paid jobs, there have been moves to involve unpaid citizens in supporting individuals in a range of activities. In adult and further education, for example, a student may support an individual with learning disabilities for a few hours a week. This promotes relationships and social network building while having little or no cost implications.

Community inclusion and building relationships

The journey into real community inclusion is a particularly difficult one for people who do not use verbal communication. Discovering the kind of activities people enjoy and supporting people to engage with other people they meet in the community are both huge challenges for support staff. Communication was central to each of the projects funded through the Choice Initiative and the issue is addressed in detail in Chapter 2.

As more people with learning disabilities are supported in community-based activities, this also has the potential for enabling people to build new relationships, though people will often want to keep in touch with friends in their day centre or other service settings. The idea of helping people develop and maintain social networks and significant relationships is new to many service providers, even though, for most of us, relationships with friends and neighbours and belonging to clubs or other community groups is an important aspect of our lives. People with learning disabilities are no different (Wertheimer, 1996).

Many services are beginning to find ways of helping people make and maintain relationships. This means a shift away from going out with three or four people, and focusing on individuals. People with learning disabilities can have an extremely busy week, packed with activities, but few real opportunities for making relationships that grow and develop.

As the projects in the Choice Initiative found, when people have very limited communication or communicate in very particular and sometimes subtle ways, supporting them to make friendships can present significant challenges.

Health care needs

Generally feeling well is an important pre-requisite for community involvement and people's ability to access community activities may be enhanced or, alternatively, jeopardised depending on whether their health care needs are receiving attention. A person with undiagnosed hearing or visual difficulties, for example, is more likely to enjoy being out and about if they are helped to overcome these problems.

There is considerable evidence, however, that people with high support needs are poorly served by the health care system. Recent government publications, including *Signposts for Success* and *Once a Day* have borne this out. A major barrier to receiving good health care is the ability to communicate about symptoms, including levels of pain and discomfort. Work done by the Kings Fund in the Changing Days project revealed a high level of undiagnosed poor health with the result that people lacked the energy and enthusiasm to get involved in community activities.

As people move away from the family home into small group homes the quality of their health care may deteriorate. Staff that support them may have had little or no training in health care. Medical knowledge is often not passed on to social care staff and people are severely disadvantaged as staff cannot act as health care advocates. Primary health care staff are likely to have difficulty in communicating with people who are non-verbal.

Listening to people with high support needs

Work undertaken by the Changing Days project (McIntosh and Whittaker, 2000) found that of 35 people with high support needs

- three-quarters were seen by others or themselves to have a greater sense of self-esteem, more assertion and greater social skills when they had access to person-centred planning or a circle of support
- people saw the circle of support as a sociable, friendly and important experience in building relationships with other people
- most had increased opportunities for leisure activities, and one in five had undertaken some form of work experience
- half the group had better social relationships
- most people continued to attend the day centre on a part-time basis and no one attended a special care unit
- many people had one-to-one support for a brief period each week
- support was increasingly tailor-made and people had a much greater say in the activities they were involved in
- most felt a closer relationship with their support worker.

On a less positive note, being offered choices could be difficult, as people had limited experience of decision-making. Mistakes were inevitably made and people learned the hard way. Difficulties included overspending, buying pets but not coping with them, and changing accommodation unsuccessfully. Some people wanted more help in making decisions and wanted to be better informed about options for activities in the community. However, most people welcomed the opportunity to be listened to, to take part in planning activities and to choose their own support worker.

Conclusion

Inclusion for all citizens is high on the government's current agenda and people with high support needs must be part of the drive towards creating more inclusive communities. The opportunities are there, but so are the challenges. When people with complex needs rely exclusively on service systems they cannot easily be part of their communities.

The next decade, perhaps as much as any, will challenge those concerned with justice and inclusion to retain their commitment to these goals and to review our reliance on service solutions to resolve issues around disability.

The policy for heightened community involvement is already solid. What remains is the really hard work of reallocating existing resources and demonstrating to one person at a time that providing inclusive community options for every person is possible and a means of achieving the national ideal of full citizenship.

Barbara McIntosh

Senior Development Manager, Community Care Development Centre,
King's College, London

The Projects' Experience
choosing community activities

People with high support needs have few opportunities to participate in the life of their local community. This is despite the fact that many services claim to operate on the basis of O'Brien's principles which emphasise community presence and community participation.

Two of the Choice Initiative projects focused on enabling people with high support needs to access activities of their choice within their local community.

Choices, based at the Markfield Project in North London, supported eight individuals on a two-to-one basis to express their wishes and access their chosen activities in the area.

> Together with his support staff, G and S, Andreas has been to garden centres, swimming pools, parks, hospitals, the library – and the local cemetery which has a beautiful pond which he enjoys. They have been out for meals and have shopped together and cooked a meal at Andreas' house. Andreas has also attended the Markfield Project's Annual General Meeting, the launch party of the Foundation for People with Learning Disabilities, and a user consultation event.

> Since joining Choices, Christine has been to the shops, the pub, the woods, cafes, the zoo, the local swimming pool and jacuzzi, as well as cooking, listening to music and having massage at home.

The Friendship Train's main focus was on providing opportunities for people to develop and maintain friendships, by offering a range of social activities in the community.

> As well as meeting in people's own homes, participants in the Friendship Train have met up for pub meals, they have been to local parks and restaurants and to the cinema, and had picnics and meals in restaurants. Some people have been to the Beautiful Octopus Club which is run by people with learning disabilities and is hosted by Heart and Soul, a brilliant and pioneering rock/soul/funk band. Participants have also joined in People to People's Umbrella evenings which involve a range of social activities.

Community participation and choice were also an important element in the other projects: the Futures Project's work with school-leavers, the Step Out supported employment project and BILD's advocacy work.

An invisible minority?

People with high support needs are more likely to have a fixed and regimented lifestyle dominated by care provision, with little or no opportunity for change or spontaneity, or access to community services, activities and events. Care is still generally provided in segregated settings.

All too often, people with learning disabilities are not part of the community. Although we've moved away from the Victorian hospitals where they were locked away, to some extent day centres do keep people within hermetically sealed bubbles.

As projects found, when they were starting out, it was difficult to gain support for individuals to access what they were offering. This was partly related to other people's expectations of this group. If people were verbal they were seen as able to make choices, but without speech they were seen as passive and disabled and as having no individuality or ability. Without someone to advocate for their needs, people could miss out on the opportunity to exercise choice in their lives.

Marsha lives at home and receives a day service four days a week, but because of her high support needs, she has no independent access to her community. Her mother is her main advocate, and after 18 months when the project staff worked closely with her, she now supports Marsha's participation in Choices. Until now, expectations for this client group meant that independent activities and social involvement were not seen as a meaningful part of Marsha's life.

As was the case with Marsha, in order to raise the expectations of families and staff, project workers needed to be able to communicate *their* belief in what they were doing and demonstrate their confidence in people's ability to communicate and make choices, despite their lack of speech.

I held an open evening with pictures, flyers, food and my own enthusiasm for the work [of the Choices project]. In this way, I became more confident about the value and potential of the work... By talking about non-verbal communication and promoting its value, we gradually raised people's expectations and got support for clients to be involved.

Wanting to be out and about

One of the projects was already offering a weekly group session for people with high support needs which focused on establishing ways in which participants could communicate their needs and wishes. From this, it emerged that some people were resistant to being in group settings, they wanted a more individualised service and were demonstrating a clear enthusiasm for being out and about.

Amy had attended the Sensory Sessions at Markfield and had become an involved and co-operative member of the group. After two years, though, she became less willing to join in the activities and refused to sit with other people at lunchtime. Instead of seeking people out and smiling and generally making contact, she would walk off from the group and push people away. After discussion with her keyworker, we concluded that she had possibly outgrown the group and was asking us for a change.

With some project participants, day services which lacked sufficient stimulus and offered a very restricted range of activities, usually in groups, could result in boredom and frustration.

Tina was attending a day centre five days a week when the project became involved in her life. The first sessions took place at Tina's day centre, partly because, at this point, her mother was concerned about Tina running off. However, these early sessions soon became very frustrating for the staff as it was clear that Tina was desperate to be outside.

This was echoed in the BILD advocacy project's units on daytime activities, which pointed out how

> lack of meaningful and interesting occupation in life can make any of us bored, frustrated and depressed. In people who find it hard to take action for themselves this may be communicated through [behaviour such as] anger and destructiveness.

Starting from home

Supporting individuals in the community meant to some extent moving into unfamiliar territory. This was often a new experience for the person with high support needs, but also for those supporting them.

Starting the session in a person's 'primary' or 'private territory' – their own room or the kitchen, for example – was often helpful, particularly in the early stages. Secondary territories such as group settings offer people limited choices, but supporting individuals in public territories offers potentially unlimited choices, both large and small.

> L, the project worker, went to Christine's house the first time they met. Christine expressed pleasure and interest in L's presence, watching her and, after a while, giving her a big grin. The next time, Christine was feeling unwell, but she allowed L to give her some massage. Christine was very relaxed, resting her feet on L's arm. A member of staff in the house who witnessed this said she had never seen Christine look so happy.

> Project workers started by meeting with Andreas at his house, emphasising that it was *his space*, that they were there on his terms and that he was in the dominant role. He wasn't being brought into a setting which was unfamiliar or where rules already existed.

Discovering choices

Trying to understand what activities a person might be interested in and choose to do was a learning experience. As Choices staff discovered, it was important to create an environment where the participant was taking the lead and where opportunities for unwittingly imposing their own preferences were minimised.

> Mirroring Andreas in his own space, with him taking the lead, would help staff learn... what things he is interested in or likes. In group settings we were more likely to try and 'get him interested' in what we were doing or things we thought he would like.

Staff were also required to think creatively, building on what they already knew about the person. When Tina's staff started working with her, they soon learned that Tina wanted to be outside and perhaps outdoors.

> The trip to the park was an enjoyable day because staff mirrored Tina, were led by her and allowed space. Tina was clearly happier than when she was in the centre and enjoyed exploring by collecting twigs.

In the Futures Project, the development of Communication Passports offered another way in which people's choices about community activities could be recorded for future use.

It takes a while to get to know Sunil. His facial expression is usually neither happy nor sad but he can display a really brilliant smile. Sunil is very responsive to stimulating environments and enjoys getting away from a contained setting. He likes visiting places where there are lots of people, he loves feeling the wind in his face and the world at large interests and stimulates him. We have recorded his likes and dislikes in his Communication Passport which he will be able to take on to his day centre when he leaves school.

While the starting-point for discovering choices must always be the individual, both Choices and the Friendship Train realised that the projects needed to familiarise themselves with the communities in which they were based. They had to build up a picture of leisure facilities and other activities in order to be able to respond to people's individual choices. The Friendship Train asked People to People's advisory group – the Big Decision – for their suggestions about possible activities. And at Choices, the project worker undertook her own research.

Widening choices

An important element in the Choices project was providing opportunities to test out the possibilities of offering choices on a wider front – not only what to eat, or what to wear, and not just either/or. Staff need to feel confident about exploring possible options which could be difficult if they were unsure about the participant's response.

Accompanying people into the community meant constantly considering what their choices might be.

During a day in the park, we would look and listen for signals from the person about where they want to be, what they want to explore further, when they want to move on, etc. We try to give them every opportunity to express their wishes and have them acted on.

Thinking about possible options to present to someone is sometimes challenging. Should we always proceed from the person's experience, offering choices within the range of what is known or familiar, or should people be encouraged to try the unknown? This was a challenge for the Step Out employment project, where very few of the participants had any previous experience of mainstream (as opposed to sheltered) employment.

Supporting choices

Markfield's Choices project was clear from the start that people would require high levels of support. Each participant was supported by two project staff. Sometimes this was because someone needed lots of physical support such as lifting, or their 'challenging behaviour' meant one-to-one would have been too risky.

At the same time, it was important that each staff member developed their own relationship with the person. Indeed, the project found that most staff wanted to spend some time alone with the person so that a one-to-one relationship could develop. At the same time, there was a clear expectation that both staff would focus on the participant (rather than talk to each other).

Having staff working out in the community, the project needed to feel confident that they would support people safely and appropriately. This became one of the key criteria in selecting staff, although other issues also needed to be considered (see Chapter 9).

A flexible and individualised approach

As mentioned above, services to people with high support needs tend to be provided according to a rigid timetable. A key element in the Choice Initiative was the provision of a more flexible service. As Markfield's project found, their original plan of providing a service one day a week was not meeting individual needs. As a result, they changed to a more flexible approach, so that clients were offered the choice of being supported during the day, in the evening or at weekends depending on the particular individual.

The BILD advocacy project too emphasised the importance of creating opportunities for activities, which took account of people's individuality.

> A citizen advocate is particularly well placed to help because the diversity and difference among people with learning disabilities means that someone committed to a single advocacy partner will have the best chance of helping that partner express his or her individualism in choosing daytime activities... Some will have preferences based on their culture, some will be young and others growing older. Opportunities should reflect this...

Going at the person's pace

Allowing someone time to develop trust in their support staff so they can go out into the community with a sense of security is essential if people are to have positive and enjoyable experiences. Helping someone get an idea, as far as possible, about what is likely to happen when they go out can help individuals cope with new experiences. This has certainly been important for Sandra.

> At times it is clear that she simply cannot trust that situations that are out of her control will be positive, regardless of who she is with. The project worker and her support worker are trying to ensure that she fully understands what is happening or going to happen so that she can feel secure and empowered about leading the pace.

People need time to become familiar with new experiences and places. These need to be introduced, repeated, explored and developed but crucially, at the person's own pace and in their own way. However much information is offered, it cannot be a substitute for actual experience. You can be shown how to swim by watching someone demonstrate how it's done, someone can tell you what the water might feel like, but you only find out what it's like by getting in the water as Tina's story illustrates.

> Tina had not been to a swimming pool for several years, but her workers felt she might enjoy the experience. On the first visit, although she did not get in the water, there were also no signs of agitation. On the second visit, enthusiastically encouraged by her workers, Tina paddled in the shallows. The third time, the workers introduced Tina to the jacuzzi by going in themselves and demonstrating evident enjoyment. On the fourth visit, Tina got into the pool for the first time and walked across to her worker.

Enabling someone to repeat experiences can give someone the opportunity to decide whether this is something they enjoy. It can also enable staff to gain a clearer picture of whether they are offering an experience which someone really likes. If someone can't say in words whether they enjoyed going to the park, for example, those supporting them may need time to find this out.

Self-expression

When is "no" really no?

In Tina's case, her workers realised that she needed time to consider whether going swimming was something she wanted to do. In some situations, however, people need to be able to refuse or reject an option which is being offered.

> You don't need to push people into doing things... nobody's saying you have to do this or that... you don't have to achieve certain targets by a certain time.

> Sandra expressed her unwillingness to participate on one day by behaving aggressively and defensively towards me. I therefore drove her home and gave her the privacy she seemed to want at the time. The following week she was calm, happy, affectionate and co-operative and enjoyed her sessions as usual.

It was important for Sandra's worker not to assume that because Sandra was saying "no" that week she was rejecting participation in Choices in general.

Missing one week's activities may be a relatively small choice, which does not have huge implications in the longer term. Knowing how to respond when someone apparently chooses to opt out completely from a project was much more difficult. When Andrew 'chose' not to continue working at the leisure centre and returned to the sheltered workshop, it was a great deal more challenging for the project staff (see Chapter 4).

It was important to record what happened in each session and to share information with carers and families, through informal conversations or more formal review meetings. Feedback also needs to be two-way. Because participants are non-verbal or have limited verbal skills, and because the contact is only a few hours a week, the project needs to know what is happening between sessions.

Mirroring

A central aim of the Choices project was to facilitate people in finding new and often individual ways to enjoy their community.

Supporting people's self-expression can make an important contribution to raising their self-awareness and self-confidence. However, this could sometimes produce interesting challenges for staff as the following story illustrates:

> Her staff do not say [to Tina] "Don't skip; we're on the high street". They support and validate her communication by joining in and being part of her happiness.

Going public

The Choices project has been able to give people:

> a flavour of the community they live in... [the chance to] feel a part of the community and let the community see that these people exist and have a right to access the community as much as anybody else.

In the borough where the Markfield Project was working, one of the objectives in the local authority's Community Care Plan was to raise the levels of awareness and understanding between staff, carers, service users and the general public; fine words, but not always easy to put into practice.

> To actually go out with somebody, especially someone who has an obvious physical disability [means] you have to cope with other people's reactions as much as the people you are working with... Staff sometimes have to explain or interpret; someone may appear to be in distress, for example, but actually be screaming with delight.

Supporting people to express themselves in the way they choose in the public arena – the 'third territory' – can sometimes raise difficult issues. When someone gets so excited in the cinema that they start making a great deal of noise, whose needs come first?

> We're having to address who has priority. Whether it's everybody else in the cinema or whether it's us all getting used to the idea that people might need to make a noise when they're doing things they like.

Trying to figure out what may or may not be acceptable behaviour in public was also an issue for Step Out.

> As part of getting to know Diane, we went out shopping together, but because she sometimes screams or bangs her head rather than using her facilitated communication board, we decided it would be helpful to work out some 'ground rules'. Diane agreed that if she screamed or banged her head, we'd leave the shop without any purchases. It's been hard to stick with this and be consistent, but we've managed it, and we've had some good shopping times as a result.

The ground-breaking nature of this work meant that staff and participants were sometimes faced with difficult situations, on the other hand, there were also many positive examples of people who had hitherto been excluded, becoming participating and interacting members of their communities.

> Most people we have had contact with have been very co-operative and very supportive ...they have understood what we're trying to do and seen value in it ...and they have made the space for that to happen. We've enabled this client group to integrate with people and services in the community... longer-term relationships are developing with people and places in the community by supporting clients and members of the public to interact.

Conclusion

A fitting conclusion to this chapter are the following snapshots from a project worker.

My overall impression has been dominated by my own impossibly subjective images of individuals. Andreas pushing his worker off the sofa, a changed character who recently made eye contact with me and took my hand for the first time. Terry enjoying football and lager; a new experience for him, but one which his peers take for granted. Amy smiling happily and now able to use public transport and enjoy community activities. Christine waving at members of the public and sharing pub meals with friends. Nicos happily sharing a bowls game and enjoying other activities. And finally my own partnership with Sandra which has given me the opportunity to witness a greater expression of excitement than I would think myself capable of if I won the Lottery!

...and these descriptions of the impact the Choice Initiative has had on two people.

Tina has relished the change in her life by enjoying local parks, cafes, pubs, swimming pools, museums and social events. Tina's mother has told us that she is laughing and smiling a lot now, something she apparently hasn't done for a long time. Now she is an active, playful young woman who is a pleasure to spend time with.

From being an aggressively defensive and isolated person, Sandra is becoming someone who enjoys being around people. Although she can still be aggressive at times, she can also be very happy and enjoy being in the community... On a visit to a horror film we were, stereotypically, getting scared when Sandra forced us into loud giggles. Sandra not only giggled; she howled with laughter, almost crying with happiness, and jabbing us with her elbow to express her hilarity.

DfEE (1999) *Learning to Succeed: A New Framework for Post-16 Learning*. Nottingham: Department for Education and Employment.

DoH (1998) *Signposts for Success in Commissioning and Providing Health Services for People with Learning Disabilities*. London: Department of Health.

DoH (1998) *Once a Day*. London: Department of Health.

McIntosh, B. and Whittaker, A. (1997) *Days of Change*. London: King's Fund.

McIntosh, B. and Whittaker, A. (2000) *Unlocking the Future: Developing New Lifestyles for People with Complex Disabilities*. London: King's Fund.

Wertheimer, A. (1996) *Changing Days*. London: King's Fund.

Choosing
work

INTRODUCTION

Employment is one of the central areas of ordinary life, providing income to meet our basic needs, and offering opportunities for decreasing dependence on others, for improving our material quality of life, for personal growth and satisfaction, and for social interaction. Current government policy emphasises helping people back into employment, including disabled people. And yet this important aspect of life is largely denied to people with learning disabilities in general, and to people with high support needs in particular.

There are a number of factors that make obtaining and holding down a job difficult for most people who have a learning disability. They often find it difficult to take what they have learned in one setting and apply it in another. The many subtle differences in task, equipment, routine and environment between different jobs and workplaces make it even harder for them. People can and do learn general work skills, but can often find it difficult to move from a training environment to a real workplace. The social demands of real workplaces are as important as the jobs themselves, but they too can differ between jobs and be difficult to replicate in a training centre, again making transition to open employment even more difficult.

All these difficulties become even more significant where people have severe or profound learning disabilities. An individual's additional physical, sensory or communication impairments can complicate the task of finding and holding down a job, with the result that few people with high support needs are found in employment. For many, a paid job is not even considered a serious option by them or their advocates.

The supported employment model

In recent years, however, supported employment has begun to offer people with a wide range of impairments the choice to enter mainstream employment. The approach is based on the assumption that anyone can be employed, if appropriate support is provided. Sometimes called the 'place, train and maintain' model of employment (Pomerantz and Marholin, 1977), it regards a job in an ordinary workplace not as the end-point, but as a necessary first step in effective training and support. By first finding a job that fits the potential employee's requirements, supporting staff are able to teach the person to carry out a *specific* job, in a *specific* workplace, with a *specific* set of routines and social expectations. The job is taught using systematic instruction, which breaks down a task into manageable steps, and has been a highly effective tool in helping people with severe learning disabilities become productive in mainstream workplaces.

The growth of supported employment

Since its inception in the US in the early 1980s, supported employment has achieved a rapid growth, with legislation and funding enabling it to operate as a mainstream form of provision, particularly for people with learning disabilities (McGaughey et al, 1994).

In the UK, supported employment services have grown steadily from only a handful in 1986 to 210 by 1995, when it was estimated that over 5,000 people were employed through services of this type. More recent informal surveys by the Association for Supported Employment (ASE) have put the number at over 7,000 (Beyer al, 1996). Supported employment is increasingly common in European countries, with ground-breaking projects emerging in Eire, Portugal and Spain, and national service frameworks developing in the Netherlands and Norway with government sponsorship.

An option for people with high support needs?

While supported employment in the US has grown, the majority of people being supported have mild or moderate learning disabilities (Kregel and Wehman, 1989, 1995). People with high support needs have been much less frequently served, which is ironic because the original supported employment initiatives in the US were largely with this group. This is changing in both the US and the UK – though more slowly in the latter case.

A national survey in Britain found that 90 per cent of people in supported employment had a learning disability and six per cent a mental illness. People with head injuries, physical disabilities, or sensory disabilities were also being supported, but each represented less than one per cent of the total population served (Beyer et al, 1999).

For people with high support needs, supported employment can be an important alternative to special care units. Projects serving this group are providing valuable insights into the strategies required to support people in paid work (Revell et al, 1994) and demonstration projects in the US have shown the feasibility of adapted forms of supported employment (eg Sowers and Powers, 1991). Some of this North American work has been with younger people, driven by concerns to improve their transition to adult life (Wehman, 1992). Britain has less experience of successfully providing paid work for people with high support needs, but valuable examples do exist including projects run under the auspices of Barnardos and Merseyside Health Trust (Wertheimer, 1996). The National Lottery has funded pilot work and research is taking place (Beyer et al, 1999).

The Choice Initiative's Step Out project under the auspices of L'Arche is making a valuable contribution to our understanding of this type of work.

Adapting supported employment to people with high support needs

Those who have worked extensively with people with high support needs have identified the adaptations that seem important in enabling them to use successfully the supported employment model. In finding jobs, the match between individual, task and environment is crucial. Exploring these through short real-life job try-outs is an important tool. School demonstration projects in the US have found that building up, over time, a good picture of the person's abilities, interests, training and personal care needs and job adaptation requirements has been significant. Person-centred planning, with its focus on pooling diverse information sources and thinking positively and creatively about people's futures, is increasingly being used to identify the crucial elements in prospective job and support needs (O'Brien, 1987; Mount, 1992).

Once the person is well understood, and an appropriate placement found, building a relationship with an employer that allows for 'job carving' (identification of parts of jobs that can be combined to make a manageable task for a person with high support needs in way that benefits them and the employer) is another important strategy. In training jobs and tasks that people with high support needs can do, the focus on 'place, train and maintain' is even more important than for other groups.

This emphasis on significant adaptation of the way tasks are done, of equipment or of environment may sometimes require skilled technical assistance; often, however, it can be achieved with fairly simple, low cost solutions in the control of supported employment agency staff.

The support offered may also need to be more flexible than is usual in supported employment. Generally, a job coach will be used to place and train an individual, fading in their involvement over time. This decreased involvement is often not possible with clients with high support needs and strategies have emerged to deal with this.

The concept of a 'support co-worker' has been used, providing long-term support to help the worker carry out their tasks (eg assisting in positioning equipment, or getting materials when they run out), or carrying out complementary tasks that make the job as a whole work for the employer (eg more complex finishing operations to complete a final product). The concept of natural support (Nisbet, 1994) has also been used to engage the employer and co-worker from the start in job design, training, and longer-term support co-worker roles.

Collaboration with others

Unlike other people with learning disabilities, for those with high support needs accessible transport, toileting, personal care needs, feeding, mobility, lifting, behavioural support may all need to be taken into account in any placement plan. Good, detailed planning, with full collaboration between families and agencies, is crucial to the success of supported employment for this group. In this country, there may be a need to involve housing staff, case managers and social workers, community nurses, psychologists or others involved in behavioural support, day service or community support workers, and Disability Employment Advisors, as well as supported employment agency staff in the planning of a job for a person with multiple disabilities.

Creating incentives

In the US, minimum wage waivers and tax credit incentives for employers have been used in some cases to support placements (Sowers and Powers, 1991). Support packages have been funded through a number of different sources such as matching federal and state monies for vocational rehabilitation and Medicaid, and local developmental disabilities agencies. While by no means perfect, US welfare benefit legislation also allows more flexibility in the transition from reliance on state benefit to earned income. There is less of a financial disincentive for people wishing to work part-time due to the challenge of a significant disability.

Removing barriers and disincentives

The UK still lacks these kinds of incentives which might encourage the employment of people with high support needs. Restrictions apply in the areas of welfare benefit, availability of, and eligibility for, skilled support resources, transport and technology. People with high support needs are likely to be receiving the highest levels of welfare benefit. Means-tested benefits, such as Income Support, are important 'passport' benefits to free prescriptions, eye tests and the like.

Entitlement to housing cost for those in residential care are high, and also dependent on welfare benefit status. The earnings, and hourly rates of pay, required to replace these incomes and entitlements if lost, are often beyond the capacities of people with high support needs, particularly if they are restricted in the hours they can work in the first instance. People in this situation can work for limited hours and retain entitlement and welfare benefit if they their work is regarded as 'therapeutic' by the authorities concerned. The amount of earned income that can be disregarded before welfare benefits are reduced or removed is low.

The national minimum wage puts a lower limit on the hourly rate of pay that can be paid, no waivers are available, and this automatically limits the number of hours people in this situation can work. Net earnings under these circumstances are restricted to £15 a week, an amount that has remained unchanged for many years despite changes in the cost of living, average wage rates, and level of welfare benefits.

The government's Employment Service (ES) offers assistance to disabled people seeking employment in ordinary jobs through Disability Employment Advisors, Disability Services Teams and the Access to Work Programme. They offer places in segregated work settings through their Supported Employment Programme offering sheltered workshop places, and through their wage subsidy scheme, the Supported Placement Scheme.

The main thrust of the Employment Service's work is to place disabled people who are willing to work over 16 hours a week and who are willing to relinquish their welfare benefit. Financial support from ES's main programmes, which could include specialist equipment, personal support in the workplace, transport, or wage subsidy to compensate employers for low productivity, are not usually available to people with high support needs because of the practical constraints on the hours they can work and the wage rates they can command.

Partly because of these restrictions, much supported employment is funded by Social Services. Provision is largely dependent on the individual community care assessment. Employment is at the margins of Social Service's responsibilities, budgets are continually under pressure, and employment provision is seldom part of funded care packages for people with learning disabilities, let alone people with high support needs. In essence, these funders do not see partial participation in the mainstream workforce as a priority, even though the government rhetoric is about helping all marginalised sectors of society to be included.

Supported employment agencies trying to place people with high support needs face other problems. People may sometimes need specialist transport if they have mobility problems. This is costly for an agency to have to fund themselves and accessible taxis and single-level buses are by no means widely available. Accessible transport is difficult to obtain from other agencies, such as Social Services, as it is under heavy demand. Getting to work is, therefore, problematic and can be costly.

Health and safety regulations rightly protect staff by insisting people needing transfers between a wheelchair and say, a work station, or to a toilet, be helped by two people or that a hoist is used (depending on the person's degree of weight-bearing capacity). While occasional transfers can be coped with in a day centre where a staff team and equipment are available, the regulation conspires against those wanting to access ordinary workplaces. Provision of two people for occasional times during the day is expensive and logistically difficult for supported employment agencies to deliver. Under the Disability Discrimination Act, employers are mandated to make 'reasonable' accommodation to assist disabled people, but hoists are expensive and their provision may be seen as 'unreasonable' when the job is only for a few hours a week.

Computing technology is advancing at an exponential pace and the use of voice synthesis and computer-controlled devices is highly advanced. Great strides have been made in using computer technology to empower people with significant disabilities in the workplace. Wheelchair technology has also come a long way, with powered wheelchairs providing significant independence for some people. The availability of these kinds of aids to people with high support needs in the workplace, however, is more rare. Some may have aids through health or other budgets that can assist in work, but funding through employment rehabilitation budgets is again constrained by the likely hours and financial outcome of the job, again creating disadvantage.

Attitudinal barriers

Perhaps the single biggest barrier lies in our low expectations and failures of imagination. It is very difficult when very few examples are to be seen locally, to imagine a person who is lying on bean bag, or being fed in a special care unit, as being in a paid job. We see jobs as complex, requiring flexibility and core skills that this person will never have. We find it difficult to imagine that being able to do very small things well can make a significant contribution and be valued by a company. Where employment resources are available there is always someone else seen as more deserving of support. They may have more demonstrable skills, they may be more able to express their wish for a job, or be an easier prospect to promote to an employer as a productive worker. We cannot believe that employers would want a person with this level of disability in their firm.

Commonly we fail to see employment as relevant to people with high support needs. Is it right to put someone into employment when they may not understand the concept of working for a wage? Is this exploitation? Are there better things that person could be doing with their time? Will they be at risk in a company? What use is a few hours work a week to anybody? These are all questions we ask ourselves, and often the answers lead us to pursue the issue no further. And yet, in small numbers, the obstacles are being overcome.

We have to be sure in our own minds that the alternatives are clearly better than employment. While day care settings can offer a secure placement with a level of personal and health care, overstretched and undertrained staff are often unable to offer good levels of stimulation to each individual across the day (Kilsby and Beyer, 1996). Good individual packages of community activities do exist, but the norm is still time spent in one building with a limited set of activities. If well designed and planned, employment can offer significant natural potential for stimulating activity, a good context for personal development, contact from co-workers, a natural pattern to the day, and some additional income.

There is a long way to go and many practical and resource barriers to be overcome before the choice of employment will become a reality to the majority of people with high support needs, their carers and advocates. The Choice Initiative does provide an image of what might be possible.

Steve Beyer

Deputy Director, Welsh Centre for Learning Disabilities

The Projects' Experience
choosing work

The Step Out project grew out of an existing supported employment scheme and Job Club. Although L'Arche has its own workshop, some of the people who used it were saying they wanted to work elsewhere. Six individuals were found work placements and, seeing their achievements, others began to say they too wanted to go out to work.

> Chris has been asking to work outside the workshop for a long time... he's not been wanting to come into the workshop... really. He's been talking with his feet. He went off and got himself a job on the building site up the road... and he now has two jobs and is over the moon. He sees himself as being the workman like his dad, with his work boots, his bag and newspaper. It's what people see around them every day; people go to work.

Believing that it was important to offer the same opportunities to people with high support needs, Step Out has focused on enabling people with severe learning disabilities to access employment.

Choosing to work

L'Arche has always emphasised the importance of listening to people who find it hard to communicate and advocating on their behalf. Thus Step Out was a response to people communicating that they wished to go out to work.

Two of the participants had already experienced work outside the community so were in a position to make an informed choice, based on existing knowledge and previous experience in the workplace.

> Four years ago, Alan had worked as a lift operator in one of the large department stores. Although, much to Alan's disappointment, the job had been terminated, this experience had given him enormous confidence. When Step Out was getting off the ground he indicated through words and gestures that he wanted to participate; he wanted a job.

For others, the pre-placement stages of the project enabled participants to gain some idea of what going out to work might involve.

> Susan had visited other people in supported employment and had attended the Job Club but she didn't really participate or show much interest. At her 'job notions' meeting, however, when her dad was saying emphatically that he didn't believe she could work, Susan leaned over, tugged at his clothes and said: "Dad, I want a job".

Choosing to go to work may have seemed relatively straightforward, but actually embarking on the process was, for most people, a daunting experience. Participants required considerable support to cope with this major change which often felt very risky (see also Chapter 8).

Addressing carers' concerns

The idea of people with high support needs going out to work can be a daunting prospect – not only for the individual but also for those around them. Project workers were aware that spending time building relationships with parents, carers and others who played an important part in people's lives was an essential stage in the project.

> We needed to work with parents so that they could trust us. There was fear and anxiety about separation... and about whether their son or daughter was being set up to fail.

Parents and carers needed information and the chance to talk to people in L'Arche about the project. There was a delicate balance to be struck. Project workers needed to listen to and empathise with the very real fears and anxieties of parents and carers. But at the same time they also needed to encourage high expectations of individuals and to communicate their own belief in people's potential to achieve.

Step Out addressed these issues in several ways. Parents, carers and significant others were kept involved and informed throughout. Psychologists, social workers and other professionals added their support and provided examples of existing successful supported employment placements. In some instances, siblings became powerful advocates.

> Andrew's mum reacted initially by expressing doubts, but his sister Rachel, along with his social worker, was able to convince her that work would be a good idea.

> Peter's sister, Kylie, has attended all the meetings and given him her full support and encouragement.

Steps to supported employment

Step Out adopted the systematic approach which has been used successfully in supported employment for a number of years. This has a number of clearly defined stages which, along the way, are designed to enable participants to develop individual preferences for employment:

- getting to know the person
- vocational profile
- job notions
- job search
- job analysis
- pre-vocational training
- job training
- reducing support.

With some adaptations it has worked well for people with high support needs in Step Out. The 'getting to know you' stage has taken longer for each person and ongoing support may need to continue. It may be less feasible for the job trainer to reduce their involvement, particularly where someone requires assistance with their personal care.

Getting to know you

As Chapter 2 discussed in some detail, building a relationship with the person was the key element, enabling communication to develop as a pre-requisite for making choices. In Step Out, this process was also important in contributing ideas about the kind of work and work setting which might be appropriate.

> Having got to know Alan, it was easy to imagine what type of environment he would enjoy working in – surrounded by people, and by noises he liked such as telephone ringing, the radio playing, the photocopier buzzing, etc.

Like all the other projects, allowing time for participants to feel more confident and secure was crucial – but perhaps particularly important for Step Out participants who would be expected to perform in a job.

Describing this as a stage in supported employment is, however, potentially misleading, and it should be pointed out that the relationship between the person and their job trainer remained central throughout the project, permeating all the activities described below.

Vocational profile

The vocational profile is drawn up by the supported employment manager, job trainer, the individual and their personal advocate who meet to discuss the vocational profile form. This looks at personal history, likes and dislikes and possible job ideas. Specific questions address issues of choice. For example, how does the person like to learn, what sort of environment do they like, how do they feel about travelling, and have they expressed any preferences about work?

> Over a period of time, certain interests of Andrew had became clear such as music, motorbikes, crocodiles, people in uniform, fire engines, police, ambulances, pie and chips, TV soap operas, Punch & Judy, travelling by bus, birthday parties and swimming... Possible work experiences became apparent. We would need to consider a job which involved clear routine, music playing, a friendly atmosphere, visual stimulation and so on.

Job notions

The job notions meeting involves a wide range of people and in this way is not unlike a 'circle of support' (see Chapter 5). The person chooses who they would like to attend and participants include the individual, their supported employment worker, the project manager, and others who play an important part in that person's life which may include family members, friends, care staff and other professionals.

Job notions sessions are positive brainstorming sessions which aim to boost the person's confidence and support them in expressing choices and preferences. Everyone contributes their own ideas, based on their knowledge of the person. The group works on the following questions:

- what are this person's strengths and attributes?
- what are their likes and dislikes?
- what are their interests and hobbies?
- what are their 'must haves' (eg time to communicate)?
- are there things they are not good at?

Armed with this information, the meeting goes on to brainstorm all the possible kinds of jobs, taking account of things like
- the kind of workplace environment
- the tasks involved
- the physical demands
- travel.

The meeting can then start thinking about actual possibilities. The final stage is to agree on *action* – what will happen next – which usually means identifying and organising one or more work placements.

Job search

At this point, the job trainer and supported employment manager begin to determine local employment possibilities which can balance the employer's expectations with the best possible match for the individual.

Like all supported employment schemes, Step Out has utilised a variety of strategies to obtain job placements. For example:
- liaison with other supported employment agencies in Liverpool helped the project to arrange placements with a major retail outlet and with a sports and leisure centre
- following up an article in a local newsletter produced by the voluntary sector led to other placements
- marketing methods included cold calling, telephoning and writing follow-up letters describing existing successful placements
- circulating potential employers with information about the project including bulletins, newsletters and annual reviews, plus publicity which the project had received from others led to an interest in the project.

> After Alan's job notions meeting, several employers were contacted including music workshops, recording studios, radio stations and a toy library. A preliminary visit to the toy library was very successful, the tasks Alan would be able to achieve with confidence were immediately self-evident, and the environment seemed one that he would be more than happy to spend time in.

Although, in Alan's case, the job search resulted in a successful placement, the inevitable negative responses from other employers weren't easy for the project. Having built up someone's confidence and identified the kind of job that would match their skills and aspirations, remaining motivated and restarting the search was sometimes difficult.

Step Out's strategy has been to assess whether the refusal stemmed from a valid concern for which there might be a negotiable solution or whether the employer was simply not open to the whole idea of supported employment. In the latter case, Step Out writes to the employer, asking them to consider their company policy on supported employment. The aim is to ask the employer to think about the issue, but not to challenge their decision about a particular placement.

Job analysis

Once a match has been made with an employer, their expectations and those of the project are explored in some detail. At this point, the job trainer learns all aspects of the job in order to be able to train the person subsequently. This is done using the Training in Systematic Instruction method, whereby a job is broken down into small steps which can be taught stage by stage. The job trainer will also go and meet the employees who will be working alongside the person to start building up a picture of how they will work alongside one another. Finally, the job trainer will start introducing the person to the workplace by making visits so that they can get some idea of what going to this particular workplace might be like.

Pre-vocational training

This builds on the person's skills and experiences and can cover areas such as travel, health and safety at work. Individuals also get the opportunity to attend the Job Club and visit other participants at their work sites.

For some people, preparation for the workplace may need to include discussing and agreeing ground rules about acceptable behaviour and ensuring these are understood.

> Peter has a pleasant and mischievous nature but can also be rather overly energetic at times. Before starting his job at a garden centre, it was agreed that he would walk quietly through the store and move around slowly.

Job training

The supported employment approach/model recognises that on-the-job training is most effective, so this is undertaken in the workplace. This is done by breaking down the job into a series of tasks which the job trainer demonstrates. The person then learns the task, supported and encouraged by the job trainer who uses physical and verbal prompts, gesture and signs depending on the individual's preferred communication methods.

> Susan's introductory morning at the nursery was successful and she was interested in learning new skills. Her first task is to greet the children after which she helps set up the toys, puzzles and other equipment. She then sets eight tables for lunch and washes up the teacups. In between these tasks, Susan is involved with the children, playing games with them, joining in singing; at the end of the morning she helps clear up. In the early days, Susan lacked confidence. Even though she set the tables perfectly, for example, she would often question whether she had got it right and needed lots of encouragement from her job trainer.

Learning to do a job doesn't always go so smoothly, however, and may indicate that this particular job match wasn't appropriate and a rethink is needed.

> Andrew's first work experience took place at a garden centre where his main task was to fill up sections of the outside area with new stock and arrange the old stock. This proved disastrous as it required him to make far too many judgements and Andrew was also not keen in taking instructions from his job trainer. The upshot was that Andrew did not know what was expected of him.

The Job Club

This part of the project fulfils a number of vital roles. At the fortnightly meetings, participants get the chance to discuss their experiences and share successes and failures. They can tell their stories, offer one another advice and gain support from their peers when making choices and decisions. Individuals can also invite people to visit their workplace.

Everyone is encouraged to participate, and the project manager facilitates meetings using a wide range of communication tools including: language, demonstration, photographs, portfolios, overheads, flipcharts, Makaton, signing and gestures.

People can come to Job Club meetings and find out what having a job might involve without any commitment to taking things further.

> When Paul first came to the Job Club, he didn't want to stay but when told he could leave he decided to remain and was interested in the photos of Chris and Andrew at work.

> Although she is not yet ready for a work placement, Diane seems to want to be at the Job Club.

The meetings provide an opportunity for people to talk about and share their 'first day' fears about a work placement. They can also hear from others how they coped with these.

Sharing their achievements with peers can boost self-confidence and can also be a good way of practising giving presentations to groups outside L'Arche.

> Susan stood at the front of the group and beamed as her work was discussed and her portfolio passed around the meeting. She said a few words about her work with the children, demonstrated how she laid the tables and joined her job trainer in singing one of the songs that she sings with the children at the nursery.

> Using slides and audiotapes, Paul and Alan both gave presentations about their work after which Paul said: "It's great they like me".

Continuing support

The supported employment approach suggests that on-the-job support can be reduced or faded out completely, once someone has learned the tasks and is more confident in the workplace. If someone has particular support needs, however, this is not always appropriate and Step Out participants are likely to need ongoing support, the nature of which will depend on individual needs.

> Although Susan is well established in her job, she still lacks confidence and needs a lot of verbal encouragement to complete the tasks. Because Susan sometimes lacks energy, the job trainer also needs to motivate and energise her at times.

> Because other people can find it hard to understand him, Chris likes me to help him communicate with them, although he no longer requires assistance with the actual tasks. He enjoys the rapport of having a friend at work with him who he can use as a tool for expressing his own personality. He often asks me to translate what he says to other work colleagues.

Supporting people in the workplace requires the support worker to negotiate a delicate balance between offering appropriate help and knowing when to stand back or facilitate individuals to do things themselves.

> Alan had a lot of tasks to learn but he picked them up quickly and needed fewer prompts with each new task, but because of his physical disability he needs hands-on support to press and turn on the machines. He also needs help to get around the workplace in his wheelchair. When he is sorting the toys, however, he likes to concentrate and has made it clear that he doesn't want to be interrupted while working.

Once someone has settled in and learned the tasks, the job trainer may also need to support and encourage other employees to communicate directly with the individual. This may be particularly important when someone has limited or non-existent verbal communication.

> When Peter started at work, most instructions were given to me. Now, however, the staff relate directly to Peter as a result of which he has grown in stature.

> As Susan's confidence has grown, she has begun to build strong relationships with the children and co-workers at the nursery where she has a job.

Relationships with employers

Step Out has worked hard to develop good relationships with the host employers and they, in turn, have generally tried to ensure that the person on work placement is genuinely treated as a member of the staff team.

The project has recognised the importance of supporting employers as well as participants, particularly in the early days. Being honest about what an employer may expect and not glossing over potential problems has helped to build trust in the scheme. Reliability and consistency on the part of project staff has further contributed to employers feeling confident about taking on an employee with high support needs.

Maintaining good relationships with employers is important, as is making contact with newly appointed managers.

> Peter had been working at the store for several months when a new manager was appointed. Unaware of Peter's placement and why he was there, he asked Peter and his job trainer to leave. A meeting was arranged where he could be introduced to Peter and find out more.

Interestingly, employers' expectations of people's abilities have often been on the low side but, as this has changed, many have been willing to invest in the process of developing people's jobs. Seeing what a person actually *can* achieve can shift an employer's perceptions about disability.

> Staff at the toy library have been very supportive of Alan, but as the manager says: "It's a two-way process and we have learned so much from Alan. He has also provided us with greater awareness and practical experience of working with people with learning disabilities. He is missed the weeks he isn't here."

Liaison with families and carers

Keeping in active touch with families and other carers was important not just in the early stages but on an ongoing basis. People need to feel supported in their choice to work and family members and carers often play a key role, sometimes in quite practical ways.

> People in Susan's house need to encourage her to be clean, smart, tidy and ready for work and they need to remind her that Anna will be coming and they will be going to the nursery.

More generally, maintaining close links can help ensure that everyone's expectations remain high and that everyone is working together to empower individuals in their choice to work.

Making choices about work

Facilitating choices about work can be particularly difficult when someone has no knowledge or experience of the world of work. At Step Out, people's experiences were mainly limited to the L'Arche craft workshops. Despite this, the project has been able to develop a range of strategies for supporting and enabling people to make real and informed choices, including

- avoiding making any assumptions about what people know or have experience of
- arranging visits to people already on work placements so people can start to get an idea of 'what's out there'
- visiting other workplaces including 'taster visits' to possible job sites.

Without sufficient information, someone may start a work placement which is not what they would really have chosen if they had understood more what was involved.

> Peter's first placement was as a handyman doing maintenance work at a training centre, but after two weeks he ran away, saying he didn't want to go back. His next job was a very different experience. Much more time and effort was invested in informing Peter what it would involve. He visited a store to see another project participant working there and was given plenty of opportunities to discuss and agree what would be expected of him. Having been supported by two people, Peter now does much of the job by himself.

It has been important to attend closely to the person and what they are trying to tell other people about work.

> Cars and motorbikes seemed to be two things that Chris was clearly interested in. He had posters of motorbikes on his bedroom wall and loved to look through catalogues on workwear. Chris now works at both a car wash and a motorbike showroom. Perhaps he is telling people that working in these places is what he truly wants to do. One thing is sure, Chris knew what he wanted but until someone had made an effort to understand him, his choices could not be met and acted on.

Supporting choice can be difficult when, like any of us, the person seems unsure about whether or not they want to pursue something. Andrew was someone who gave these kinds of mixed messages in his first placement and, in fact, subsequently chose to move to another job eventually where he seemed much happier.

> Andrew would wait for me outside his house, he'd have his uniform on and would have signed that he was going to the store in a very positive fashion to his mum. At times he would also hit his face, refuse to take off his coat and on two occasions actually vomited.

Andrew was saying "no" to a particular job, but having moved to another workplace where he seemed more comfortable, he subsequently chose not to go to work. That was a difficult choice for his supported employment worker to accept, even though Andrew's communication of his wishes was abundantly clear.

> He started saying "no job" and hid his work bag. "No! No! No work!" he repeated. He has returned to the L'Arche workshop. So what made Andrew change his opinion about work? Had something happened at work? Did he feel he was missing out in L'Arche? Did he not like the physical labour the job entailed? All this is speculation, but one thing is for sure – Andrew's choice has been listened to and met. This has allowed Andrew a voice within supported employment – albeit a voice that is difficult to hear.

So Step Out has supported people's choice not to work or to work fewer hours, but it has also supported the choice to work more hours or expand the job.

> A few months after he started working at the toy library, Alan reached out and touched the photocopier, indicating that he would like to develop his skills in that area. This was arranged at his six-month review. Alan thoroughly enjoys what has become his favourite task and which also increases the time he spends with colleagues.

The impact of Step Out

Being empowered to choose mainstream employment has, without doubt, changed some people's lives. The role and aim of Step Out has exceeded that of finding supported employment. The project has been called to respond to participants' growth as individuals.

> Susan has blossomed since joining Step Out. She seems to care more about herself, she feels more valued and this in turn has increased her self-esteem. She has started to emerge from her withdrawn state. She reaches out more to other people and she has developed some good relationships with people her own age.

> I think because of our relationship, Chris was able to understand that I was there to help him but not necessarily do the job for him. He had the choice as to whether he wanted to do things or not and after a few months he grabbed that with two hands. He really thought: "I like being here and maintaining and polishing these bikes... and that is all part of my image, part of me... and I can show that I work here and you don't" kind of thing. You can see it in the way he is... he's really quite proud of working in the motorbike place.

Alan is somebody who has really benefited from being out and about in the wider community, meeting new people and having the responsibility of a job. He enjoys telling people in the house and at the day centre about the toy library. He has made some strong friendships with co-workers and with his support worker, and he spends more time with others in his house and less time alone in his room.

Spreading the word

Project participants have been powerful advocates for supported employment for people with high support needs. They have presented at a national conference and given talks to school-leavers at a special school. Chris was also filmed for a BBC *Lifeline* programme featuring L'Arche.

Alan uses an overhead projector and photographs to help get across what he wants to say and is supported by his job trainer who encourages him to speak by asking trigger questions to which he can respond with rehearsed phrases.

Chris' speech can be difficult to understand but his job trainer interprets for him – although Chris doesn't always like to be interrupted when he is talking! Like Alan, he also uses a range of communication aids including overheads, video clips and his portfolio to illustrate what he does at work.

Conclusion

Step Out has successfully supported people in unpaid work placements, usually for one or two sessions a week. For the present, paid work remains a dream. The issue has arisen because Alan has indicated his wish to be paid for his work at the toy library.

A further key issue is whether it is worth focusing so intensively on employment, or would it be equally worthwhile supporting people in other community-based activities? Is there something unique or special about the workplace?

It is difficult to generalise. As L'Arche found, "each person has had different experiences; being in work is about you, about what you bring to it and how involved you become… it can bring new relationships and new opportunities and can open new doors. It can also test and challenge". In that sense it mirrors some of the experiences of other projects, particularly Choices at Markfield.

The project staff were very clear that most participants felt there was something important about the workplace, being given the opportunity to contribute to society, to be productive, to be part of a team, have goals and be responsible – and realising that they can be all these things.

Beyer, S., Goodere, L. & Kilsby, M. (1996) *Costs and Benefits of Supported Employment Agencies: Findings from a National Survey.* Employment Service Research Series R37. London: Stationery Office.

Beyer, S., Kilsby, M. and Shearn, J. (1999) *The organisation and outcomes of supported employment in Britain.* Journal of Vocational Rehabilitation, 12:137-46.

Kilsby, M. and Beyer, S. (1996) *Engagement and interaction: A comparison between supported employment and day service provision.* Journal of Intellectual Disability Research, 40: 348-58.

Kregel, J. and Wehman, P. (1989) *Supported employment for persons with severe handicaps: Promises deferred.* Journal of the Association of Persons with Severe Handicaps, 14: 293-303.

Kregel, J. and Wehman, P. (1995) *At the crossroads: Supported employment a decade later.* Journal of the Association of Persons with Severe Handicaps, 20: 286-99.

McGaughey, M.J., Kiernan, W.E., McNally, L.C., Gilmore, D.S. and Keith, G.R. (1994) *Beyond the Workshop: National Perspectives on Integrated Employment.* Boston, MA: The Children's Hospital, Developmental Evaluation Clinic.

Mount, B. (1992) *Person-Centred Planning. Finding Directions for Change in Personal Futures Planning.* New York, NY: Graphic Futures, Inc.

Nisbet, J. (1994) *Natural Supports.* Baltimore, MD: Paul H. Brookes.

O'Brien, J. (1987) *A guide to lifestyle planning* in B. Wilcox and T. Bellamy, (eds) *A Comprehensive Guide to the Activities Catalog.* Baltimore, MD: Paul Brookes Publishing.

Pomerantz, D., and Marholin, D. (1977) *Rehabilitation: A Time for Change.* in E. Sontag (ed), *Educational Programming the Severely and Profoundly Handicapped.* Reston, MA: Council for Exceptional Children.

Revell, W.G., Wehman, P., Kregel, J., West, M. and Rayfield, R. (1994) *Supported employment for persons with severe disabilities: Positive trends in wages, models and funding, Education and Training* in Mental Retardation and Developmental Disabilities, 28: 256-64.

Sowers, J. and Powers, L. (1991) *Vocational Preparation and Employment of Students with Physical and Multiple Disabilities.* Baltimore MD: Paul H. Brookes.

Wehman, P. (1992) *Life Beyond the Classroom: Transition Strategies for Young People with Disabilities.* Baltimore, MD: Paul H. Brookes.

Wertheimer, A. (1996) *Changing Days.* London: King's Fund.

Choosing
friends

INTRODUCTION

Loving another person deeply means risking rejection and abandonment, so it can be an extremely painful investment. The downside to relationships is that we can get hurt and we have the power to hurt others. On the other hand, we only have to examine our own experiences of forming close bonds with others to appreciate the flipside to pain. Perhaps this is why, for many vulnerable people, and particularly those with learning disabilities, there is a huge shroud of protection set up to prevent the forming of deep and lasting natural relationships.

"I love you" is probably the most emotionally charged phrase in any language. We all want to feel loved – whether by parents, children, a lover, a partner or friends. We hear the words, not only as they are spoken but also through action, through touch and through the way our eyes and thoughts meet. Feelings of love and warmth are more often than not expressed without speaking.

This chapter explores the development of friendships and relationships within the lives of people who often find themselves excluded from opportunities to make and sustain strong connections, and who are wrongly considered incapable or unworthy of deep love. Yet the need to love and be loved is universal. This is reflected in popular music and the best lyrics speak to and for many different people. Everyone would have some experience to contribute to a chapter such as this. Love can transcend barriers of age, culture and academic prowess. Although there is research to suggest that we often look for people like ourselves, there is counter-argument to suggest that opposites can also attract.

Micheline Mason (1990) tells us that disabled people even more than others cannot survive without relationships and services can be designed to support relationships rather than damage or replace them. Projects such as the Friendship Train, which set out to expand and develop people's social networks which might ultimately result in lasting friendships, are extremely rare. In too many services for people with high support needs, the notion of friendship is not recognised. Whilst other needs may be met with high quality buildings, the presence of real friendships in people's lives may not even be considered as an issue to be measured in any assessment or quality review. Only with the advent of person-centred planning have services begun to ask "What part do other people play in this person's life?".

In many residential care settings, it has become commonplace for support staff to be considered as 'friends'. There is a widespread complacency in human services that paid relationships are *all* that people need and little thought given to the results merits and pitfalls – not least the fact that staff turnover is often extremely high, leading to constant loss in relationships. It is little wonder that some people give up on relationships. Changing such entrenched attitudes and practices calls for a major paradigm shift – a new way of thinking. The Friendship Train highlights some of the key factors and many of the obstacles which need to be overcome.

The role of support staff can be changed. This is strongly evidenced in the work of David Schwartz (1992) where he discusses in detail the importance of looking closely at the values base support staff operate from and the need for major change in human service systems in the UK.

The introduction of Direct Payments (Holman with Bewley, 1999) has begun to give some disabled people the power to make their own choices about who is employed and the roles they fulfil. Where individuals write their own job descriptions and recruitment criteria, it is becoming increasingly common to use support staff to enable and facilitate a range of different relationships to flourish. The role focuses on serving rather than controlling people's lives, though for people with high support needs this can only happen with the assistance of others. For some people this commitment has been fulfilled through an advocate or a group advocating powerfully on that person's behalf such as a circle of support. Some parents and other family members are also bringing about a deliberate change in attitudes.

Love does make the world go round. That feeling of being valued unconditionally by someone who knows us intimately gives an incredible feeling of well-being and joy. The invitation to live within the life of others forges bonds of acceptance and belonging which cannot be achieved through other means. Human beings are inherently social, they seek out attachments to others, and the emotions engendered by friendships and relationships with people we care about enables our self-actualisation. We use these close ties to measure who we are and how we are doing and we look for reciprocal ways to communicate our feelings. The need to attract others into our inner circle is powerful driving force and can motivate many of the decisions we take in life. It is only through our relationships that we can truly develop the gifts which make us unique and different. In this sense, love is very powerful. Given the immense importance of relationships in our lives, it is astonishing that in human service provision, where people are paid to care and support others, so little attention is given to this.

People who have high support needs and who may not communicate with words share the same needs for friendships and close relationships as anyone else, though this is sometimes not apparent to others. A person, who has experienced rejection, perhaps in infancy, perhaps later in life, may have found it so painful that the only way they can survive that experience is to push other people away and withdraw into themselves. People who have spent all or most of their lives in institutions have sometimes made close relationships, as Ben's story testifies. But for many others, life has been isolated and bleak in the extreme.

As well as meeting people's basic requirements for food, warmth, clothing and shelter, services have poured resources into things like medication, risk prevention, behaviour modification, manual handling and supervision. Despite the knowledge that the only real safeguard that works for vulnerable people is found in the sustaining of a circle of people, who love and care beyond costs and benefits, there have been only limited attempts by care providers to resource this.

Respect for the relationships people have formed while using a particular service is of paramount importance. Service systems have unthinkingly broken up friendships. Sarah and Mark were parted by the residential service paid to provide care because they were considered 'bad news' together. Fortunately Sarah's circle of support reunited them two years later, and to this day they have a sound and happy marriage.

Hospital resettlement programmes have contributed to these ruptured connections. People who shared their lives for 20 or 30 years have been separated permanently and completely.

Ties and connections will break down unless they receive attention. For people with high support needs, this requires careful thoughtful planning by others – not only an awareness of actual or potential relationships, but practical support which might involve arranging transport, making phone calls, negotiating with other care staff or with families.

As we journey through life our experiences and interactions offer many opportunities for the development of relationships. Participating in family life and in various communities in our neighbourhoods brings us into contact with people we may choose to engage with more closely. Spending time in the same place as others promotes familiarity and proximity, key ingredients for a nurturing environment where relationships can flourish. The important qualities of friendship such as the gifts of time, kindness, loyalty, belief, acceptance, trust, faithfulness and communication can develop over time and are sustained by the emotions felt between people.

Changing the values base from one where people with complex disabilities are seen as 'perpetual children' and unequal citizens, to one where each individual is seen as unique and of equal value is the starting-point. This is extremely difficult to establish in entrenched services, which subscribe to the medical model of disability. If 'differentness' is seen as 'lesser than' or 'inferior to' it is difficult – or even impossible – to believe that relationships with people with high support needs can be reciprocal, yet "reciprocity is at the heart of all relationships of any emotional depth" (Bayley, 1997: 29).

Undoing myths and stereotypes, understanding current disability politics and changing mind sets are the positive outcomes of good disability equality training led by disabled people.

Families who have had little support from professionals and who have been told not to have overly high expectations for their son or daughter may, not surprisingly, have wished to protect them from failure and disappointment. This, together with the heavy burden of care which may be involved, can make it difficult for families to facilitate friendships outside the home. Young people who are taken by bus to and from special school every day and otherwise spend all their times within the family, simply do not have the same opportunities for making friends and deeper relationships as other adolescents.

Encouraging and supporting participation with people who share common interests will lead to the development of friendships. Whoever supports the individual needs to be highly skilled and motivated in providing the required quality and sensitivity of support. All too often, disabled people are subjected to trips into the community which enable support staff to visit places *they* are interested in, chat with one another, and generally follow their own agendas. It takes skilled facilitation to firstly discover the gifts and interests of the individual, the hooks which will enable their participation and contribution.

> *For Ben, his interest and deep pleasure in popular music, the graceful way his body moves and the enjoyment he takes in the freedom of movement when he is released from the confines of his fairly cumbersome wheelchair, are definite gifts. In the local hi-tech gym he has found good music, open floor space, opportunities to exercise and relax, and lots of young people his own age with whom to make connections. His two support workers have figured out which two regular weekly slots bring him into contact with the friendliest crowd and have ensured his regular attendance on those days. Within a few weeks, his presence was missed when he took a day off and people began to call him by name. His own joyousness in the activities acted as a magnet and people were drawn into conversation through the expert intervention of Ben's support assistants. Over time he was joined in the bar after his workouts and gradually began to make three important friendships.*

Despite Ben's particular gifts and his friendly outgoing personality, these friendships would not have ignited without facilitation by others. Many of Ben's peers have sat out their days in special needs units, their eyes hazy with a vacant gaze.

Focusing on recruiting staff who can facilitate opportunities for friendship must become a priority for services which provide for people with high support needs. Writing new job descriptions, offering training in communication, support without control, community building and person-centred planning are achievable, practicable steps which can lead to changed services.

The shift from acquaintance to friendship is often subtle and yet the result of that shift can make a huge difference to the quality of daily life. Feeling truly valued by someone who knows who you are, the good and the not so good qualities, and appreciates your worth without judgement, creates a platform for growth.

Every person should have friends. The right to love and to feel loved is fundamental. Love isn't always complex or messy; it is also the quest for finding ourselves, the opportunity to release our spirit and our spiritual potential. The capacity we have for love is not based on our intellectual, physical or emotional development, and disabled people, people with learning difficulties have as much need for fulfilment as anyone else. Although such information seems too obvious to state, it is surprising to look at the myths and stereotypical beliefs which are tightly held by countless ordinary people. Such discriminating values underpin action which often excludes disabled people from opportunities to develop and sustain deep friendships and, in some cases, strong family relationships.

Because of their differences, people can be viewed as incapable of opening their hearts. Barriers are erected which prevent opportunities to participate in ordinary community life and which control and limit opportunities to meet people and sustain relationships at more than a peripheral level. Such barriers can be created subconsciously out of fear and ignorance, or for more sinister reasons, to oppress and persecute people for their apparent difference. There is a huge issue of justice to overcome if we are to address the poverty of relationships many people with learning difficulties and other differences experience, within our human service systems and other communities.

Some people have the ability to believe in miracles occurring in the most unlikely surroundings. Colin is one such person.

> *After 30 years in a long-stay hospital, Colin had been labelled as "having severe intellectual impairment and homosexual tendencies". His life experience had provided less than average social skills and he didn't have access to many personal relationships. Yet when Simon walked into his life one day, initially as a staff member, he opened his heart and warmly welcomed a friendship which has endured over several years. He has developed a warm and giving personality without the excesses of anger or withdrawal which others may use to conceal great pain. The responsibilities of friendship, to talk, to listen, to hold, have been easy for him. The desire to engage with, accept and care for Simon in a strong platonic friendship, despite such constricting circumstances was perhaps the 'miracle' he always said he was waiting for. Now living independently in his own home, with good support, the barriers have eroded and his particular gifts can be received by a wider circle.*

The pain of isolation and loneliness are arguably the greatest disabilities faced by people and the impact is often devastating and debilitating, leading to self doubt, confusion, despair and hopelessness. Creating the bridge between separateness and belonging calls for great understanding and support.

Because we don't live in an inclusive world, a world where love is safe, there is a need to tread cautiously when setting the foundations of bridge building. Several ways have emerged to redress the personal experiences of exclusion and the public failure to include people of difference.

To have people to call on, friends to share our troubles and joys with, family and close allies who will assist us and be there for us through whatever life throws up – most of us aim to achieve such aspirations. To have none of this in place, to be so isolated that our lives feel disconnected and barren, is a difficult place to start. If someone has experienced a life of broken ties and connections, separation from family and friends and limited experience of support to develop new relationships, then it is probably going to take some time to turn their life around.

Befriending schemes and advocacy schemes have made a difference in some cases in the development of friendships, but the weight can be a heavy one for the befriender or advocate who can often become oppressed too when professionals put obstacles in their way. Paid relationships, where staff members share close personal activities and environments with the people they are paid to support, can also offer new possibilities. However, career moves, organisational rules, demands of others in need of support and unequal positions of power can all contribute to inadequate true chances for deep and lasting friendship to develop. Paid workers often perceive that they are a friend to the person they support and yet may not consider having that person on their own personal guest list. Excellent paid support may well be the necessary and desirable outcome from such relationships whilst in addition, the pursuit of real, natural and unpaid friendships can be assisted by workers.

The growth of self-advocacy groups in the UK has also provided opportunities for disabled people to spend time together, often away from service settings. Although not always the case, groups have often included people with high support needs amongst their membership. Although not the primary focus of self-advocacy, these developments have enabled people to make new friends and widen their social networks.

Circles of support (Wertheimer, 1995) have provided a simple path to the establishment of strong and meaningful interactions and ultimately the development of lasting friendships. A circle of support is essentially a simple way of bringing about personal and social change. The person who is experiencing isolation invites others to meet with them on a regular basis to dream about a more desirable future and to take action to make this happen. Members of a circle might include family, friends, colleagues and other associates who have agreed to support the focus person in friendship and care. No one in a circle is paid to be there except where the resourcing of a paid facilitator is deemed necessary. The aim of the circle is not to create another dependency model of care, but to allow people the free space to think and plan creatively and to problem solve in a way which enables the person and those closest to take and maintain control. Sharing the tasks between a number of people means that no one person feels overburdened and everyone begins to learn new skills. The employment of a facilitator should only ever be short-lived. Members of the circle can quickly develop confidence to undertake this and any other roles. For people who use alternative communications systems it is important for all members to learn the most appropriate forms.

The circle acts as a catalyst and a conduit for social relationships to develop. It is not there to provide an alternative service. People involved in the group may choose to draw in their own friends and family thus extending everyone's social networks. Most of us search out friends who can satisfy at least one of our needs. In a circle, the greater the need for change, the more people and wider diversity we need to engage.

The emotional support offered by a circle of support is invaluable. Knowing that people are there to be called on, to listen, to advise and to celebrate achievements makes a tremendous difference to our sense of self worth.

It is this blend of practical assistance and emotional support along with companionship and fun which makes the circle so vibrant. Sustaining the momentum and continuing to offer hospitality and reciprocity in each other's lives are key issues for the circle to focus on. Not losing sight of the individual's dreams and aspirations, however, is the most important dynamic. Ultimately the circle takes the shape of a set of natural interactions and once inclusion in community settings, participation in purposeful activities and the right balance of support and care are firmly established, it may not be necessary to meet up so regularly. Once the bridge from exclusion to inclusion is constructed and there are more people involved in the person's life, even as things change and one or two individuals lose interest or move away, there are still sufficient relationships to build on and develop.

In creating inclusive communities where people are welcomed for whom they are, where friendships are based on love and not on paid exchange, and where our differences are seen to be gifts, we each will experience new ways to think and behave.

The barriers to inclusion, the blocks to equal and healthy relationships will gradually erode. It may not always be easy to find the gifts in people who have learned to communicate through aggressive, difficult or compulsive behaviours. It will take a great deal of empathy and tolerance to look beneath the layers and discover the person within.

Believing in the notion that each person has gifts to contribute, a reason to belong and a purpose to enhance the lives of others helps us to perceive people differently. Our diversity and creativity will make communities rich and rewarding places to live within. Changing our beliefs is no easy task though, and there is a great need to share the leadership and learning towards equality.

Whatever role we play, whether it involves completing a family, becoming a dreamweaver, a bridgebuilder, a listener, an excellent support worker, a lover, a friend, we can work at all of our relationships in the spirit of love.

Mandy Neville

Chief Executive, Circles Network

The Projects' Experience

choosing friends

Friendships are something which most people take for granted in their lives. As the introduction to this chapter reminds us, the need for others reflects a basic and universal human need for attachment. However, people who have difficulties communicating with others will, almost by definition, find it difficult to make and sustain friendships. Whether someone lives with their family or in a service setting, there are likely to be few people who could truly be described as friends and few, if any, opportunities to *choose* friends.

> People [with high support needs] have very little choice in terms of making friends and people have very little opportunity to go out and make friends... all different kinds of friends and relationships that I might take for granted in my own life.

For people to make friends, they have to be in places and situations where there are other people with whom they can communicate and interact – the workplace, college, pubs, clubs, leisure facilities, sporting facilities and so on. A person who spends most of their time at home or in a day centre will have limited opportunities. Whether living in residential care or in the family home, many people with high support needs live very isolated lives.

Recognising the importance of friendship in people's lives, the Choice Initiative funded People to People to set up the Friendship Train, a project which would specifically address this issue by finding ways of breaking through the barriers behind which many people with high support needs live in isolation.

People to People had always emphasised the importance of relationships in their work with people with mild learning disabilities. With the Friendship Train, however, they were breaking new ground, entering largely uncharted territory. The project set out to challenge some conventional notions about friendship and to explore how people with high support needs could be facilitated and supported to make friendships.

Steps to facilitating friendships

The Friendship Train encountered many challenges in working with other agencies and organisations, but also had to struggle with finding the best way forward itself – how to find the optimum frameworks, processes and strategies which would offer people the possibility of friendships.

Important lessons emerged in the early days in relation to the recruitment of potential participants and the framework adopted. The original idea was to bring together a number of young adults in a fortnightly 'friendship' group. Each person would be accompanied by a 'significant person' in their life – a parent, key worker or support worker, for example. Facilitated by two project workers, the group would provide an opportunity for individuals to explore the idea of friendship and express their wishes about the kinds of leisure activities they would like to pursue. People would then try out new activities with one or two others in the group in between the fortnightly meetings on the assumption that enjoying shared activities might lead to the development of friendships.

The project used several recruitment strategies including handing out flyers at day centres and residential establishments and circulating local voluntary and statutory agencies with information. Visits were also made to people where there had been an expression of interest. The aim was to stimulate interest from individuals and their carers. This could be difficult when the project worker was unsure whether someone understood what the Friendship Train was offering.

> She was reluctant to make eye contact with me, but seemed happy for me to sit next to her. Every now and then she would shout loudly. I had made some large pictures of different activities and showed them to her but they didn't make much of an impression.

> At no point was there any eye contact with me while I was discussing the group with him and his key worker. He seemed to want to keep his distance from me.

> She was very keen to find a boyfriend. She considered this to be the main reason for joining the group. We spoke briefly about the need to have patience with this sort of thing.

In the event, although there were numerous expressions of interest, no one attended the first group, necessitating a rethink and a different approach, since neither the recruitment strategy nor the proposed group structure seemed to be what was needed. Although this first phase was disappointing for the project staff, it was a useful learning exercise and important lessons emerged which are described later on in this chapter.

Drawing on what had been learnt in the first phase, the project decided to try out some different strategies. Contact was established with residential homes. Initial calls were made to ten establishments plus follow-up calls. Contact was also made with individuals living with their families. As a result, ten people had some contact with the project.

Three small groups of about three people in each were to be linked within their communities. Some progress was made, but proved difficult to sustain. There was confusion on the part of some family carers who saw these gatherings as primarily enabling them to link up with each other. With hindsight this is not unexpected, given the current emphasis on family support, and given that the project was inviting them to attend these groups with their son or daughter.

The final – and more effective – phase started when the project decided to work towards facilitating friendships between several people already linked to the project, together with several isolated individuals in group homes where staff were known to be supportive. This approach had a number of important features:
- the focus was on a smaller number of individuals, including people who had been specifically identified as isolated
- project staff worked more directly with individuals rather than trying to facilitate and support individuals and carers
- rather than inviting people to come to a group, the Friendship Train became peripatetic, moving into where people were rather than expecting people to come to the project base
- more time and energy was devoted to developing effective means of communication which reflected individuals' particular ways of expressing themselves
- more resources were invested in building trust and confidence among support staff.

Understanding friendship

Friendships for people with high support needs have to be respected and nurtured. For many people, this had not happened. It was therefore unsurprising that the project workers discovered that

> friendship proved a very difficult concept to convey and there was limited understanding of what friendship meant. Their social networks and opportunities were much more restricted than those of more able people with learning disabilities.

So how do you convey the concept of friendship? Is it something, which can be learned? After all, most people learn about relationships through experiencing them. What the Friendship Train did was to offer people the kind of social activities where friendships between people might begin and develop and the workers' role was to be present to facilitate those possibilities emerging.

> The role of the two facilitators was very much hands-on, meeting people, making connections with people, going out into the community... there are often people who might struggle with communicating what they want to do or who they might be friends with... the facilitators' role was very much about sitting with people, watching people, listening to people, picking up on how different people communicate...

What people were being offered could perhaps be described as a 'pre-friendship' space where individuals could, in their own time, explore the possibilities of friendships. The project also did this by inviting people who had expressed interest in the Friendship Train to come along to People to People's regular Umbrella events.

> The Umbrella evenings are places where people do simple things like going to a pub... buying a drink, maybe buying a drink for someone else... these evenings are a simple opportunity to go out into the community. People may come as a group or by themselves. And really it's just a chance for people to sit undisturbed and talk to one another.

The project workers attended meetings of People to People's Big Decision advisory group whose members include local service users. This group helped inform and develop the project's work generally and was able to contribute the ideas about friendship.

➡ *Friends are close. Friends remember your birthday.*

➡ *It is harder to make friends if you cannot speak.*

➡ *It's difficult to keep in touch with people; sometimes they move away.*

➡ *Sometimes friendships can lead to a relationship.*

Many members of the Big Decision were particularly concerned about isolation and loneliness in the lives of people with high support needs, while recognising that these were issues they were facing in their own lives.

The project staff themselves also struggled to understand the meaning of friendship, particularly when it involved individuals who had little or no verbal communication or whose expressive language was limited.

> This was difficult to unravel; presence is different from interaction and participation. Dimensions of friendship are very difficult to measure, observe and assess. Someone who has communication difficulties does not necessarily initiate and maintain friendships easily. People in the groups have had parties and have wanted to invite other people but this is not necessarily indicative of friendship.

However, through carefully observing people, they could make some reasonable guesses.

> Often eye contact, facial expression and body language as well as gestures would indicate or suggest some level of closeness or association. A number of participants registered pleasure and enjoyment when familiar faces appeared at events.

The cultural context for friendship

Being based in an area which is ethnically and culturally very diverse was a particular challenge for the Friendship Train. Establishing contact and building trust with some of the parents proved difficult and this may have had something to do with the fact that both project facilitators were white British women.

The bulk of the people involved in the Friendship Train, including service users and support workers, were from black and minority ethnic communities. With hindsight it would have been helpful to have employed workers whose ethnic background mirrored this, who could have worked alongside the two facilitators.

The project staff were also aware that concepts of relationship and friendship are to some extent culturally defined and work with family carers (and support staff) needed to take this on board. There are very powerful stereotypes about people from different cultures, as well as stereotypes about people with learning disabilities and the project probably needed to address more specifically how these could be challenged.

Recognising the importance of friendship

Individuals with high support needs can have difficulty in grasping the concept of friendship, but staff and carers may also find the idea difficult to take on board. An increasingly important part of the Friendship Train's work was advocating for people's right to friendship.

> Seeing people as real people with real needs in relation to emotions and friendships... friendship seemed to have become another taboo area. The new idea seemed to have challenged existing services as well as families and the support structures they have built up over time. Occasionally the idea of friendship was perceived to be much needed respite for the carers rather than [something] for the person themselves.

The Friendship Train had been offered as 'a good idea' to local services but, despite general expressions, of support, they did not always want to be involved. There was an important lesson here; the project needed to advocate more forcefully to overcome the scepticism or inertia of service providers. It was perhaps also the case that the project needed to be promoted; in clear terms of what it was offering *individuals;* promoting a broad general message about the importance of friendship was clearly not sufficient.

Where families were concerned, there were other reasons perhaps for their failure to engage with the project, including lack of suitable transport, fear about personal safety if going out after dark; and older parents being less mobile themselves. The project was initially asking people to come to meetings with a carer, and for already over-stretched family carers, this probably made it a less feasible option.

Faced with a lengthy period when the project was achieving few tangible results, sustaining a belief that the project was addressing a fundamental but unmet need in people's lives was an important dimension. The need to hold on to a vision of what someone's future might be like, while keeping one's feet on the ground is graphically described by one of the project workers when he went to meet David, a potential participant.

> I wanted the project to solve all of David's problems and felt the weight of the project's aims fall on me. I felt anxious and excited that the Friendship Train would be able to deliver choices, opportunities and possible new friendships into David's life. A small part of me thought that maybe this project could change everything and introduce a new way of doing things to [his keyworker] and new meaningful friendships to David.

Friendships between project workers and participants

As some of the other chapters have described, relationships between individual participants and project workers were often very important, enabling participants to communicate, make choices and generally exercise more control in their lives. But could these relationships be described as friendships?

Two people spending time together doesn't necessarily result in a friendship developing: it may, or it may not.

> People are individuals; they strike up different relationships with people... sometimes you become great friends with a person and it's a real friendship... but working with some people, it's actually a professional relationship and they keep quite cool and quite distant, but they're very reliant on you – and you are reliant on them.

Some staff-participant relationships in that particular project did develop into mutual friendships, possibly because the organisation where the project was based emphasised reciprocity and a strong belief that people with high support needs are people who have something to give to others.

Friendship and service systems

People with high support needs will be more dependent on services to provide care and as the Friendship Train realised, that can make them hard to reach.

> They have more structure around them... they need more people to work with them and support them... but it means that it's often hard to reach people... With the best of intentions, people are often buried alive in the services that are there to support them... As an outside agency it was often quite difficult to make real contact.

The pervasive culture of many services places little value on friendship. Indeed, services can unwittingly break up friendships or fail to support people in existing relationships. Someone can be moved into a group home and have no say about whom they live with. A person can be moved to another home, or even another area, with no consideration of how this might affect existing friendships. Changing to a different day service can mean losing contact with people who may have been part of your life for many years.

Brainstorming within the project about their differences with services, while necessarily subjective, helped identify some of the possible reasons why the Friendship Train was difficult to get started. Existing services usually operated to a fixed timetable, aimed to provide security and reassurance, and tended to be prescriptive. A project like the Friendship Train, on the other hand, aimed to be non-prescriptive, to offer choice and flexibility; and required active commitment and a willingness to take risks on the part of the individual participant as well as from significant people in their lives.

Despite these difficulties, one committed support worker or family member could make all the difference and where project workers identified staff who seemed supportive, they sought to build on this.

> A lot seemed to boil down to the support person's motivation, insights and values. One man is always up to coming out [with the Friendship Train] but he has a really committed keyworker.

The project also encountered support staff who, though sharing their aims, shared something of their clients' isolation and marginalisation, and found that it could be difficult to open a door in the very structures which offer much needed care and support in people's lives.

> Derek communicates using body language, facial expressions and sounds, and gets around in a wheelchair. He shares a house with three other people with high support needs, and his keyworker, Kevin, was excited about the project becoming involved with them. Although Derek had his own car, Kevin had difficulty finding places to go to which Derek would enjoy and the project worker sensed their isolation. However, although Derek and Kevin were invited to a series of social events, they never showed up; a telephone call revealed that things at the house had been busy, it had been hard to get out, but they did still want to. After a further silence, the project again made contact to discover that Derek no longer had his car which made it almost impossible for him to get out.

An important lesson for the project was that services have to be worked with, rather than in spite of, and seen not as the problem but as part of the solution. This meant working with managers and support workers, respecting their ways of supporting people and sharing skills and knowledge.

> We thought that friendship should come from outside these [service] structures, but we now know that it needs to be timetabled from within, especially as it will largely depend on [those who provide and run services] for making it happen.

Furthermore, projects such as those in the Choice Initiative may not be ongoing so it is parents and key workers who will have to support and sustain friendships.

Transport is a common problem for people who need help to get around and the Friendship Train was no exception, whether people were living with their families or in residential care. The project did not offer help with providing or arranging transport which made it difficult for some people to get to events and with hindsight maybe this was a mistake. Other projects, whose budgets included provision for transport costs, did not experience the same kinds of problems so future schemes need to consider this when planning, especially if activities in the community are involved.

Did people make friends?

As mentioned above, measuring friendship is difficult but as a result of the Friendship Train, eight people were meeting in small groups and engaging in social activities together, mostly in the community. Most were previously rather isolated, lacking meaningful friendships and social contacts. Although it would perhaps be unrealistic to claim that they constitute a group of friends, they are, according to the project manager:

> A small gang of people who belong, so that when they go out they have a sense of association. They are a peer group. Overall, those friendships which have been established could best be described as casual social acquaintances.

Although the project often found it difficult working alongside services, the need for and value of friendships almost certainly gained a higher profile amongst local service providers.

A *developing friendship*

The manager of Rosalind's house was concerned that Rosalind never went out and she was seen as very much a loner. Project staff were told it would be difficult to involve her as she never appeared to show interest in other people or remember their names. Rosalind finds going out to new places difficult, but she came to some of the Friendship Train activities, and despite finding it difficult to communicate with other people she seemed to enjoy being there. Care staff had told the project that Rosalind would leave or not even turn up if she didn't want to do something, but she turned up most weeks and always stayed. After a few months, her house manager commented that she was talking about other people for the first time. Meanwhile, project staff sensed that Rosalind was making some contact with another participant, Barbara, and were delighted when they heard that they had begun meeting outside the Friendship Train. Barbara, an African woman in her early twenties, shares a staffed house with five other women whom she relied on most for friendship. She had had some contact with People to People over the years but had not been able to meet her need for social activities so she was very keen to join the Friendship Train. After a few meetings she began to make eye contact with Rosalind, laughed and seemed pleased to see her. Rosalind, on the other hand, was still rather withdrawn and didn't really give her a lot of eye contact. The two facilitators meanwhile talked generally about the idea of exchanging telephone numbers, modelling ways of initiating friendship.

When the Friendship Train went out to the cinema one evening, Rosalind wasn't there and Barbara mentioned her name a couple of times. One of the facilitators suggested it might be worth telephoning her or asking someone to do that on her behalf. A few weeks later, over a ploughman's lunch, Barbara indicated that she had rung up Rosalind and they were going to meet up. Project workers were aware that maybe these two woman wanted some kind of affirmation of their tentative moves towards making social contact, but that their potential friendship needed to develop away from the gaze of staff.

One project included amongst its aims: [enabling people to] "integrate with people and services in the community [and] develop friendships".

Going out into the community with people, staff found themselves acting as advocates, intermediaries, friends and carers. As the project manager reflected, though, friendship was quite an idealistic issue. They recognised people's lack of friends, but were also aware of the emotional difficulties which could make it difficult for people to develop friendships. Some individuals could only relate in ways which were overly intense and experienced by others as demanding, while others shrank away from any kind of overtures from other people.

The flexibility of friendship

Although the Friendship Train focused on supporting the development of friendships between people with high support needs, the project's experiences also raised issues about friendships with staff. As services become more individualised and people spend less time in large congregate settings, staff are increasingly likely to be working on a one-to-one basis with increased opportunities for people to get to know each other and for friendships to develop. This, however, may challenge the not uncommon view that staff are professionals and should maintain a professional distance from service users.

Promoting friendships between people with high support needs was challenging, given that most people had difficulties with verbal communication. With hindsight, involving people with lesser support needs might have led to more interaction between participants.

Conclusion

The Friendship Train set out to "increase the possibility of friendships of their own choosing" for a group of people with high support needs and it proved to be one of the most difficult and challenging areas of the whole Choice Initiative. At the same time, it produced some of the most valuable insights into a complex aspect of life – and one that challenges many non-disabled people!

The most important lessons that emerged were that enabling people with high support needs to make *and* sustain friendships is not easy. People with learning disabilities are always, almost by definition, poor. When planning activities, it was important to find activities that were relatively cheap. It requires a strong commitment, consistency, creativity and persistence on the part of those in a supporting and enabling role, particularly when there seems to be little tangible progress.

It takes time for two individuals to get to know one another, to build a relationship and find ways of communicating with and understanding one another. People who are isolated and lonely and who have difficulties with communication may find this less easy.

An individual approach is essential and basing the project around group activities may not necessarily have created the optimum context for friendships to develop, particularly for individuals who had little or no verbal communication. However, when the project was redesigned and smaller and more flexible groups were meeting, this did provide a more viable framework in which friendships might blossom.

Bayley, M. (1997) *What Price Friendship? Encouraging the Relationships of People with Learning Difficulties.* Wootton Courtenay: Hexagon Publishing.

Holman, A. with Bewley, C. (1999) *Funding Freedom 2000: People with Learning Difficulties using Direct Payments.* London: Values into Action.

Mason, M. (1990) *The Breaking of Relationships.* Paper produced by Parents for Inclusion and the Alliance for Inclusive Education.

Schwartz, D. (1992) *Crossing the River: Creating a Conceptual Revolution in Community and Disability.* New York, NY: Brookline Books.

Wertheimer, A. (ed) (1995) *Circles of Support: Building Inclusive Communities.* Bristol: Circles Network.

Choosing
how you live

INTRODUCTION

The choice of a place to live is arguably the key to many other opportunities for choice. It allows or inhibits access to occupation, education, leisure, community, friends and family. The home, its location and the support received there are all crucial to make choice in these other domains of life possible.

The Foundation did not receive any suitable funding applications for projects which would focus on choice of a place to live. Nevertheless, we are highlighting the issues in the introduction to this chapter, because

- very few people with high support needs currently exercise any degree of choice about where they live
- the fact that very few grant applications for housing projects were received suggests that this may be an area receiving too little attention
- all the Choice Initiative projects found that where people lived and how they were supported could have a significant effect on the degree to which they empowered to make choices.

Leaving home

The Mental Health Foundation's report, *Building Expectations,* recognised the considerable potential demand for housing and the need for choice.

> We believe that people aged 18 or over should be given the option to leave the parental home if they wish. Those agencies purchasing and providing services should ensure that policies are not based on an assumption the people with learning disabilities should remain in the family home. *(1996: 4.6)*

Government guidance is less prescriptive, suggesting that people should be helped to remain at home for as long as they and their families wish but recognising that sooner or later a move will be necessary (DoH, 1992).

A central plank of government policy is the promotion of independence, but whereas this may have a particular meaning for older people and those with physical disabilities, its significance for those with learning disabilities is less obvious. If people are to be supported to live in their own homes, it isn't clear if this is really to be their own home or the parental home. Are they to stay with their families for as long as possible, or are they to gain their independence at a reasonable age like most other people? On what basis will these decisions be made?

All too often, the reality is that nothing happens. Families are confused and unsure or they avoid the issue, and services only respond to crises when families can no longer cope. Meanwhile, government and local authorities do not have to dip into their own pockets for alternatives to family care or actively plan for people's futures.

If the values underpinning service developments reflect concepts such as choice, empowerment and independence, then service planning must accept that people should be able to choose whether they remain with their families; and if their preference is to leave home, then consideration needs to be given to when and how this should happen. Without the assumptions there is no means for framing national service guidelines or performance measures.

Like everyone, people with learning disabilities have different views on how and where they would like to live. Some want their own front door, others may welcome the chance to live with others. Some want to live near their families; others want to move away. Much is made of the need to involve people with learning disabilities and their carers in making decisions about a move, but in practice these major decisions are not always well planned. Where the person does not communicate verbally, it is even less likely that their views and wishes will be considered, even though, as the following experiences of one parent and her son illustrate (Alaszewski et al, 1999), people *can* make their views known in other ways.

> When John was being moved around trying to find a residential spot for him, we tried three residential homes and although he can't talk, he can't tell us, he walked out of one and he just wouldn't entertain it and the social worker said: "Well he's voted with his feet, hasn't he!" Now, when we came here, he didn't know this place from another and the first thing he did was settle himself down on the settee and he looked as if he was at home. The atmosphere had obviously got to him.

Choice in learning disability services has traditionally has been limited. Although formal guidance has increasingly emphasised the importance of planning around individual needs and preferences, in practice people continue to be slotted into available service. Even today, 70 per cent of placements are in some form of residential care – not infrequently on the basis that because someone has high support needs this can only be met in a residential care home or specialist unit. Do we believe that this really represents what so many people want? In practice, choice is limited.

Limitations on choice of a home

Current government thinking about where people should live is reflected in *Modernising Social Services* (DoH, 1998) which suggests that services should enable "those assessed as needing social care support to live as safe, full and as normal a life as possible, in their own home wherever feasible".

Changing priorities

Service development over the last two decades or more has concentrated on moving people out of long-stay hospitals with substantial funding being transferred to make this possible. Further shifts in policy and funding are now required. First, the focus must move to addressing the needs of the next generation living at home with their families. Second, expenditure on hospital resettlement projects must continue to ensure provision is made for succeeding generations who have not been hospitalised. Third, the process of moving people from hospital is very different from that of planning moves for those leaving home.

Lack of information on need and demand

Building Expectations recommended that government should agree a clear definition of unmet housing need; and that local authorities should establish a register of unmet housing need among adults living in the parental home or elsewhere (Mental Health Foundation: 1996: 4.7-4.8). Although this housing need has been subsequently acknowledged elsewhere (eg Audit Commission, 1998, DETR DoH, 1997, DSS, 1998) no progress has been made in tackling these issues. The proposed national standards (DoH, 1999) on learning disability services could include a requirement to collect basic data on population in a simple form. This could cover

- a profile of the population for whom services may be provided from a register or database which is maintained and updated annually
- number of people with learning disabilities
- where people live now
- number of people living with carers over 60
- number thought to be in need of a move from the parental home or existing unsatisfactory placements
- numbers receiving a joint housing and social services assessment as required by S47 of the NHS and Community Care Act 1990
- a map of existing accommodation, identifying gaps in provision
- the type of new places and support required.

With this information, planning could take place, with the possibility of greater choice.

Clarifying national and local objectives

There are currently no proper targets or standards for which to aim. From survey and planning figures (Mental Health Foundation 1996) the shortfall of places is about 25,000 places in England and Wales (or 50 per 100,000 population). A further 10 new placements a year for every 100,000 population are also needed to take account of an ageing population. Local variations are significant (Emerson and Hatton, 1996) but with nationally agreed targets, it would be possible to compare the performance of individual local authorities. The government agenda for efficiency and *best value* gives the opportunity now to set better standards and compare services.

If separate data were available for people being supported in their own homes and those receiving residential care, it would also be possible to measure progress towards meeting the government's aim of promoting independence.

Information used to plan future services is often poor, yet the population of people with learning disabilities in an area is relatively small, not particularly mobile and not subject to rapid change. Using an agreed common form of data collection, local consortia could then compare population data, needs, service costs, performance indicators and benchmarks.

Pressure on services

There is evidence (Audit Commission, 1996) of pressure on services, stemming from the enhanced role of social services following the 1993 transfer of funding responsibilities from health authorities.

Pressure on existing services has a number of knock-on effects: emergency and crisis services are full; new places are not being created at the required rate; inappropriate placements are unavoidable; services to meet particular needs (eg people from ethnic minorities; people with high support needs) are lacking; and eligibility criteria are increasingly excluding those with fewer support needs.

Little is done to encourage individuals and their families to make planned moves rather than waiting until a move from the parental home becomes the only option. Eligibility criteria give a low priority to non-urgent, non-acute cases.

Lack of a range of options

A range of services has been developed over time, including larger local authority residential care homes, smaller group homes, specialist residential units and housing tenancies with care and support. Registered residential care remains the most common option, but even this option tends to be standardised because staffing regime for shared homes and the minimum requirements for registered homes influence the style of provision.

Not only does this limit choice; it also excludes people with high support needs who are often forced to move out the area because nothing appropriate is available in the immediate locality. Supported housing, which can provide a more individualised and flexible approach to accommodation and care, is still only a minority option. According to local surveys, only seven or eight per cent of people with a learning disability have their own home.

There is a lack of self-contained housing options, limited access to tenancies in ordinary housing with support, too many crisis moves from family homes and lack of information about those placed out of the district. Many are dependent on elderly relatives, about 40 per cent with carers over 60 (Watson and Harker, 1993).

Residential providers are rarely able to offer a truly flexible range of provision. A new and updated version of 'core and cluster' should be developed to offer greater variety. For example, 24-hour cover should be available to individuals with tenancies in self-contained accommodation. A person with high support needs should be able to live on their own – with round-the-clock support – rather than be forced to share with others if this is not their preferred choice.

The need for information

Individuals with learning disabilities and their families need to plan for the transition from living at home. Accessible and reliable information is a pre-requisite for making informed choices and can help reduce fears and lack of confidence about the future.

Improving planning and commissioning

When considering how to increase choice in housing, it is important to consider the role of care management. Recent research (Harker and King, 1999) suggests that
- individual assessment does not necessarily inform strategic or service planning
- purchasing decisions are based less on choice than price and eligibility tests
- services tend to be static rather than dynamic
- information about individual preferences is limited
- choice is confined by lack of knowledge of services available.

None of this makes for an efficient market system. Concentrating on casework and individual assessment can neglect aggregate assumptions required for planning. To make the market more efficient, individual demands and choice must influence the planning and provider parts of the market. Otherwise care management is only a gatekeeping mechanism, inhibiting response.

How can individuals express their wishes and how can choices be made?

Choosing where to live – a checklist

What do you want?

- *Where do you live now?*
- *Who do you live with?*
- *What do you like about living there?*
- *What don't you like?*
- *What help do you get at home?*
- *Can you get extra help if you need it?*
- *Have you ever thought about moving?*

Why do you want to move?

- *To move to a better area?*
- *To move to a better house?*
- *Need more space?*
- *To be near friends or family?*
- *To be more independent?*
- *Can't stay where you are?*
- *Other reason(s)?*

Who do you want to live with?

- *Other people?*
- *Friends?*
- *On your own but with help?*
- *In a house where you know other people?*
- *With your family?*
- *With another family?*
- *Another possibility?*

Where do you want to be?

- *In a town or in the country?*
- *In a busy or quiet place?*
- *Near friends or family?*
- *Within easy reach of shops or other centres?*
- *Near your work or day service?*
- *Other ideas?*

Who could help with your ideas?

- *A social worker or care manager?*
- *Housing advisor?*
- *Parents or friends?*
- *People First?*
- *Mencap or other voluntary organisation?*
- *A specialist advisor?*
- *A housing or care provider?*

(King and Harker, in press)

The decision making process

It is helpful to consider the points on the checklist when seeking to improve the decision-making process. Despite the increasing emphasis on individual choice and user involvement, assessment and purchasing decisions are generally a matter for the authority arranging and funding residential care or housing and support. Eligibility criteria and decisions about individual needs are largely guided by professional judgement and affordability. Authorities are required to take account of their resources in making these judgements. There is sometimes scope for individual choice, but the consumer does not hold the budget. Choice too often still depends on the assistance and discretion of professionals.

To increase the chances of people with high support needs exercising choice about where they live, a number of things need to happen:

- priorities for services need to be set in national and local strategies
- assumptions about transitions to independence must be part of these plans
- national and local plans must take account of rising demand for community-based services
- authorities should plan with individuals and their family carers to assess needs and decide on suitable options for the future
- a wider range of housing and support options should be developed to extend the scope of existing services
- information should be provided for people with learning disabilities and their families about the options for housing and support
- individual preferences should be given a greater weight in decisions about where someone will live, whom they will live with and how they will be supported
- practice guidance is needed, which promotes person-centred planning approaches
- people with severe, profound and multiple learning disabilities are particularly restricted in their choice and practice guidance should emphasise the importance of enabling them to express their preferences
- the supply of housing should be improved through closer collaboration between housing departments and providers
- more flexible forms for supporting people, which are both responsive to individual need and which also satisfy the requirements for security and safety, need to be developed.

The home environment and opportunities for choice

Even if people with high support needs still face major hurdles in choosing where they live, what happens 'at home' and how a person is supported in and from that place can make a real difference to their lifestyle.

It is important to recognise the significance of choices possible at home: about who you live with, who provides support, meals, furnishings, possessions, visitors, leisure activities, household routines, whether to move. Services have begun to pay more attention to how individual wishes can be accommodated within the requirements of a managed service, although there are still too many examples of institutional practices in the residential care sector.

As the Choice Initiative projects found, where people lived and how they were supported often had a significant impact on the work of the projects and what they were able to achieve. This was true for people living with their families as well as for those in residential care settings.

Even making initial contact can be difficult. Families may lead very isolated lives. The demands of caring for someone with high support needs can leave little time or energy for activities outside the home, added to which there may be practical difficulties with getting around if someone has severe physical disabilities.

Residential care homes may be physically located in the community but can still be isolated, even in densely populated urban environments, particularly if homes are anxious not to stand out in any way. Blending in can mean invisibility.

Because of a lack of alternatives, people with high support needs are often forced to spend long periods of time at home, particularly in the evenings and weekends. However, family members or care staff can advocate for an individual by constantly seeking out opportunities in the community which improve their quality of life.

For an individual whose communication is limited or largely non-verbal, having another person who is committed to supporting them in their chosen lifestyle can make all the difference – a person who acts as their personal champion, (Smull and Burke-Harrison, 1992: 8-9). A personal champion is not necessarily a key worker or house manager, but where this is the case and they move to another job, this can jeopardise someone's participation in activities outside the home. It can be as basic as having someone who is going to ensure that transport is available, or that other staff in the house know you are supposed to be going out at a particular time and make sure you are ready.

Residential staff and family carers play a pivotal role in the lives of people with high support needs. They can support and reinforce a person's choices – or they can sideline them – and the experience of the Choice Initiative projects really brought this message home. Where and how we live are fundamental to our ideas of autonomy and choice. Where we live can be confining or it can provide opportunity.

Maurice Harker

Consultant with the Housing and Support Partnership

The Projects' Experience
choosing how you live

No single project in the Choice Initiative focused specifically on enabling people with high support needs to access the housing and support of their choice, although BILD's *Pathways to Citizen Advocacy* training materials included a unit on *Choice in Where to Live.* Nonetheless, the places where participants lived and the lifestyles within those homes frequently influenced their ability to make choices and bring about changes in their lives.

Choosing where to live

As *Pathways to Citizen Advocacy* points out, for most of us, choice of a home and whom we live with are the foundation of our lifestyle. It is said, "home is the place we return to", where we come back to after a day's work or generally being out and about in the community.

For people with high support needs, where and how they live may play an even more important part, as they are likely to spend more time at home and be more dependent on other people. At the same time, as Maurice Harker's introduction to this chapter elucidates, their housing options are likely to be very restricted. People with high support needs who have moved out of the family home still too often have no choice about where they live, who they live with, and how they are supported at home.

BILD's training materials highlight a number of key issues about housing which advocates the need to consider:

- although housing choice is to some extent restricted for everyone, unnecessary restrictions are often placed on people with learning disabilities – for example, funding is available for a residential placement and alternatives are not considered; because someone has communication difficulties, it is too much trouble to take the time to understand their choices
- individuals with high support needs require time and assistance to understand what the various options are in order to make an informed choice
- advocates may need to acquaint themselves with relevant housing legislation.

Citizen advocacy highlights an issue which is central to the advocacy relationship but also lies at the heart of choice and empowerment for people with high support needs: the importance of recognising and acting on the person's own choices, particularly when the preferred option may not be one we would choose for ourselves, or indeed for the other person.

Angus, who had high support needs, had been moved from a long-stay hospital to a home in the community which he shared with 11 others. He thrived there and arrangements were made to move him to a bungalow where, together with two others, he would continue to be supported by care staff. He also began a citizen advocacy partnership at this point. Following this move, however, Angus's behaviour and personality changed dramatically; he was obviously depressed and on occasion was violent towards others. Although the relationship with his advocate was only in the early stages and communication was not yet well developed, the advocate was able to form the opinion that despite all the apparent advantages of the bungalow, Angus preferred the large house where he had been living before. As a result, Angus returned to live there and soon reverted to his normal and friendly self.

The impact on choice of where people live

In all the projects it was evident that where individuals were living, who they lived with and how they were supported within that accommodation, had a significant impact on the degree to which the projects could support people in exercising greater control over their lives. Staff and other carers could play a very positive role. Alternatively, their attitudes and actions could restrict individual choices and opportunities.

Staff and carers as gatekeepers

Two projects had the potentially difficult task of having to start from scratch when it came to establishing relationships with staff and carers and gaining their trust and co-operation. Although one of these projects was working with a pre-selected group of young people, the other project had a different starting point and, initially, had sought to offer opportunities to a wide variety of individuals across quite a wide area.

> Local services were divided into patches and systematically contacted both directly and indirectly by linking into existing forums. Flyers profiling the project were also circulated.

As they realised during the first year, trying to establish contact with a large number of houses and individuals was simply not practicable. It diluted the effort required for outreach work, leaving project workers with insufficient time and energy to invest in building good working relationships in a more focused way with fewer people. As a result, their strategy shifted to working with a smaller number of residential homes and individuals.

> The focus became a group of residential homes in one area enabling the project to network and make contact with managers of houses... Partnership with services and support from managers and staff was required to establish and maintain positive contacts. Without this support it would prove very difficult to facilitate choice in the area of friendship for someone with high support needs.

Even when people are living 'in the community', they can remain largely hidden from others. For one project worker, trying to find someone's home highlighted how difficult it could be to help someone connect with the world outside.

> When I went for my initial meeting with Derek and his support worker, it took me hours to find his house because it was tucked away in a complex of new housing. His house didn't have a number, unlike most of the other houses.

The outreach work with residential homes and families often took longer than had been anticipated, partly because initial attempts to communicate with 'gatekeepers' were, as one project manager found, "either totally ineffective, misunderstood or never received".

Even when contact was established, staff and carers could adopt a gatekeeping role in relation to the project, screening and restricting access and contact with potential participants. Workers sometimes made subjective choices about who *they* felt could or could not benefit from the project, rather than working with project staff to reach a shared decision – and, most important of all, one which involved the person themself.

From the projects' cumulative experiences, it is clear that for outreach work to be effective, there must be opportunities for face-to-face meetings with potential participants and their carers before any one-to-one work can begin. Well-prepared meetings are essential and, as one project found, providing transport to and from home to the meeting means there's a greater chance that people will turn up.

Working with residential staff and carers

Two projects worked with individuals who were already involved with the organisation where the project was based (although in one case, this did not apply to all participants). This often made it a great deal easier for the project workers to build good collaborative relationships with residential staff and family carers.

The projects were generally working with individuals for only a few hours a week so gaining the trust and respect of those who were the main and continuing providers of care and support was crucial. It also made it easier for project staff to use the home as a starting point when getting to know an individual.

Working with individuals in their own homes

Project staff often found it helpful, particularly in the early stages, to spend time with people in their own homes, observing them in a familiar environment and building the relationship in an environment where they felt comfortable and where there were fewer distractions than out in the community.

House staff sometimes made a very positive contribution, by welcoming project workers into the home, rather than seeing them as an unwelcome intrusion.

> Andreas' house manager was particularly supportive of the aims of Choices and was instrumental in maintaining the relationship; she provided a positive environment where the Choices staff felt comfortable working from his house.

However, there were also instances where staff were less positive about the project's involvement.

> S was recruited to work with Amy, and started by working from Amy's house. Although they had 12 sessions, it was difficult as staff in the home did not support Amy's wish to be more independent and frustrated S's attempts to facilitate Amy to feed herself, for example. S eventually decided she could not continue.

Shared hopes and expectations

The Choice Initiative is based on the belief that people with high support needs, people unable to communicate verbally, *can* make choices in their lives and can exercise some control over their lifestyles. The projects which comprised the Initiative did not disprove this in any way but highlighted some of the ways in which this can happen for individuals – and ways in which choice can be restricted or denied.

Perhaps it came as no surprise, however, to find that staff and carers did not always share these beliefs. Staff employed to *care* for people described as having *very special needs* or being *high dependency* may not find it easy to see these same individuals in a more positive light. Families who have been told that their son or daughter will require *lifelong care* can also find it difficult to believe that this person can, despite their support needs, make choices. Projects encountered a range of responses.

> Terry has a very supportive mother who, when the project made contact with him, was already accessing his local football club, pubs and restaurants in addition to a day service; he had an independent advocate and good long-term relationships.

> The project has only been working with William for a few months but his worker is constantly surprised by the depths of his ability and his attempts to communicate. However, other people have somewhat disabling attitudes towards William, and his mother and father want to protect him from any possibility of failure. Their "he will never do that" attitude is pervasive and follows William in everything he attempts, but as they and others notice that William can do things, their attitudes are beginning to change.

Staff leaving

A member of staff leaving and moving elsewhere can have a major impact on individuals. They may have relied on that person to advocate for their needs. They may have been the person in the house who they were closest to. They may have relied on that person to be their interpreter if they had significant communication difficulties.

When staff left or were not replaced immediately, this could leave an individual with no one advocating for their involvement in the project.

> Although the project had found it difficult to gain support for their aims from Amy's care manager and house manager, the departure of her key worker, J and no immediate replacement, together with the imminent departure of her care manager, meant the work would be unlikely to succeed. Amy now receives increased day care from the local authority instead.

Conclusion

All the projects were working with people on a part-time basis and sometimes interventions were time-limited so it was important for project staff to work in collaboration with other staff and carers including those who were supporting people at home. This was not always easy, particularly where there were personnel changes, or staff did not necessarily share the same values and aspirations for people with high support needs. Where house staff were interested, supportive and eager to work with project staff, however, this could have many positive spin-offs for the individual concerned.

Alaszewski, A., Alaszewski, H. and Parker, A. (1999) *Empowerment and Protection.* London: Mental Health Foundation.

Audit Commission (1996) *Balancing the Care Equation: Progress with Community Care.* London: HMSO.

Audit Commission (1998) *Take your Choice: A Commissioning Framework for Community Care.* London: Audit Commission.

Department of Health (1992) *Social Care for Adults with Learning Disabilities,* LAC (92) 15. London: HMSO.

Department of Environment/Department of Health Circular (1997) *2 Housing and Community Care: Establishing a Strategic Framework.* London: HMSO.

Department of Health (1998) *Modernising Social Services.* London: Stationery Office.

Department of Health (1999) *A New Approach to Social Services Performance.* London: Department of Health.

Emerson, E. and Hatton, C. (1996) *Residential Provision for People with Learning Disabilities: An Analysis of the 1991 Census.* Manchester: Hester Adrian Centre.

Emerson, E. et al, (1999) *Quality and Costs of Residential Supports for People with Learning Disabilities.* Manchester: Hester Adrian Centre.

King, N. and Harker, M. (in press) *Making Housing Choices.* Brighton: Pavilion.

Mental Health Foundation (1996) *Building Expectations: Opportunities and Services for People with a Learning Disability.* London: Mental Health Foundation.

Smull, M. and Burke-Harrison,S. (1992) *Supporting People with Severe Reputations in the Community.* Virginia, USA: National Association of State Mental Retardation Directors.

Watson, L. and Harker, M. (1993) *Community Care Planning: A Model of Housing Needs Assessment.* London: National Federation of Housing Associations and Chartered Institute of Housing.

Choice
through citizen advocacy

INTRODUCTION

In recent years, advocacy has come to the fore as a way of ensuring that people who in other circumstances might experience intolerance, discrimination and neglect are provided with an opportunity to speak up about issues which matter to them. Typically, this involves decisions which are likely to have major consequences, for example, consent to medical or surgical procedures, or representation within the criminal justice system (Lord Chancellor's Department, 1997, 1999). However, the role of advocacy extends to participation in more mundane choices which are nevertheless significant to the person concerned, for example, choosing where to live, and with whom. For people with a learning disability, the growth of advocacy services has been prompted by a number of inter-related events: first, the elevation of individualism as the pre-eminent ideology in industrialised countries; secondly, the closure of long-stay hospitals and the emphasis on community based services; and thirdly, the recognition that even within community settings, many people need help to make their voices heard and to participate as citizens.

Advocacy is best understood in terms of what it seeks to achieve, rather than by what advocates and advocacy groups actually do. The list of different kinds of advocacy is already long and seems to be rapidly growing: self advocacy; citizen advocacy; peer advocacy; group advocacy, crisis advocacy; complaints advocacy; resettlement advocacy, etc. While each of these types of advocacy has a slightly different focus and involves different ways of working with service users, they all seek to provide a common set of outcomes for people with a learning disability. Atkinson (1999) summarises these as follows:

- empowerment: gaining or regaining the power to take decisions and make choices in all areas of life, large or small
- autonomy: to be a self-determining person; to be seen as unique
- citizenship: to safeguard rights; to support the person in being a fully fledged and respected citizen; and to counter injustice
- inclusion: involving and welcoming people into groups and communities, on the basis of equality of opportunity and access.

Others have placed more or less emphasis on one or two of these outcomes depending upon the context in which advocacy is provided or the particular user group concerned. For example, the Scottish Health Advisory Service suggests that "in the context of the NHS, advocacy means enabling people, so far as possible, to make informed choices about, and to remain in control of, their own health" (1998: 5). While for the National Youth Advocacy Service it means speaking up for people (or enabling them to speak up for themselves) and trying to help them make changes in their lives, particularly by representing their views, wishes and needs to decision-makers and remedying breaches of human rights (1999: 2).

The term citizen advocacy is usually applied to a "one-to-one relationship between a volunteer spokesperson and their disadvantaged partner" (Atkinson 1999). In the context of learning disability, the disadvantaged partner is usually someone who finds it difficult to speak up for themselves, possibly because of shyness or the lack of social skills, but more usually as a result of severe or profound learning disability, very limited communication skills, and possibly additional disabilities such as poor hearing or vision. (In the rest of this introduction, the term 'severe learning disability and complex needs' is used as a short hand summary to describe this group of people).

Atkinson (1999) describes a variety of supports, which might be provided by an advocate:
- emotional support and friendship
- instrumental support, for example obtaining services
- encouragement to speak for themselves
- representing the interests of the partner, as if they were their (the advocates) own.

From this brief summary it is clear that citizen advocates working with people with severe learning disabilities and complex needs must operate in a number of distinct social roles. First, citizen advocacy is based upon the development of a relationship between the advocate and his or her partner. Not only is this a pre-requisite for emotional support and friendship, but it is also the foundation for providing other instrumental supports. For example, enabling a person to speak for themselves when they feel able to do so, and being available to offer additional support when they encounter obstacles or lose confidence, is a sophisticated tutoring skill which has been extensively documented among parents and teachers. While it is a skill which some parents appear to develop naturally, adults working in formal settings such as schools benefit from specific training (Wood, Bruner and Ross 1976; Wood and Wood 1984).

Applying what might be described as the golden rule of citizen advocacy, "representing the interests of the partner, as if they were the advocates own", implies another role and a different set of interpersonal skills. It is important to emphasise that the interests of the service user refer to their wishes and aspirations, notwithstanding what others might see as social and psychological limitations arising from their disabilities. The first task of the advocate is not to make judgements about the person's *best* interests, but to divine as clearly as possible what they see as that persons *own* interests.

For the advocate working with someone who does not use spoken language, this implies an ability to infer complex psychological states on the basis of non-conventional methods of communication and the interpretation of behaviours which may not be used in any deliberate sense to communicate at all. Establishing what different behaviours mean in this situation parallels the task faced by parents trying to make sense of the behaviour of newborn infants (Grove et al, 1999). Typically, parents achieve this seemingly insurmountable problem by establishing interactive routines by which, over time, individual behaviours acquire a shared meaning. However, whereas parents have the benefit of engaging with their infants soon after birth, citizen advocates face the additional obstacle of learning to understand behaviours which have been shaped as a result of experience over many years. It may, therefore, be extremely difficult for advocates to understand the significance of particular behaviours unless a third party, for example, a family member or carer, can explain what it means.
It is also important to recognise that infants and their caregivers gradually acquire a communicative repertoire over a period of weeks and months of one-to-one interaction. It seems reasonable to suppose that a citizen advocate might take a similar period to work out the personal interests of a person with a severe learning disability and complex needs.

When *representing* what he or she believes to be the person's interests to other people, the citizen advocate is required to adopt another quite different role. Rather than establishing a long-term relationship with one person, this role involves the advocate in speaking on behalf of their partner in a variety of social settings. Moreover, it is expected that the task of representation will be carried out with conviction and determination – as if the person's interests are indeed the advocate's own. Considering the wide range of settings in which advocates might need to perform this role, they are likely to need a wide range of social and diplomatic skills – concise exposition; rigorous analysis of complex issues; strategic thinking; tact and sensitivity.

Lastly, to be effective, it is essential that the process of representation is carried out in a completely unbiased manner. This means that the advocate does not use his or her personal values or preferences to judge the rectitude of the partner's interests. Similarly, the advocate should be completely free from any personal or professional commitments which might affect his or her ability to provide *independent* support for the advocacy partner.

It should be clear from this brief discussion that very demanding expectations are placed upon citizen advocates and the groups which have been formed to co-ordinate and manage their activity. The remainder of this introduction summarises five of the major issues which will need to be addressed if citizen advocacy for people with severe learning disability and complex needs is to flourish in the future.

The meaning of choice

At the heart of advocacy is the promotion of choice and support for independent decision-making. However, the manner in which choices are made by ordinary non-disabled people is far from straightforward, and the situation is considerably complicated when one person seeks to understand or interpret the preferences expressed by a person who does not communicate using spoken or written language, or a conventional sign or symbol system.

Choosing is a complex psychological process which in ideal circumstances involves understanding the options available, having some knowledge about the likely consequences of pursuing different options and being able to execute the preferred option either directly or via an intermediary. In practice, most choices are made with partial, incomplete or inaccurate information about both the full range of options available and their associated outcomes. Executing a choice is very often a gradual process subject to monitoring and review, and most everyday choices can be suspended or reversed if the consequences do not meet expectations. In summary, choice-making in most everyday settings is not a set of categorical decisions with pre-determined consequences, but part of a continuous process of adjustment and readjustment to the world we live in.

Much social interaction which occurs between parents and their infants, or between carers and people with severe and complex learning disability, promotes this procedural type of choice-making. Nind and Hewitt (1994) provide numerous examples of the way in which social interaction creates opportunities for making choices and for discovering the consequences of selecting different options. Typically, the settings they describe are made 'safe' by the limited 'cost' attached to poor choices and by the opportunities provided by the carer to constantly renegotiate choices.

In contrast, the choices for which advocacy is regarded as most relevant are of a totally different order. They tend to involve relatively complex issues which are likely to have a significant impact on the life of the person concerned. Very often there is a high 'cost' attached to poor choices and subsequent renegotiation is difficult or impossible. It is important to consider carefully whether or not a person with severe learning disability and complex needs, who has previously only experienced procedural choices, is able to understand what this kind of categorical choice involves.

A related question concerns the extent to which even experienced and well intentioned advocates can infer what a person with severe learning disability and complex needs understands of the options and consequences of choice. Grove and her colleagues (Grove, in press) have provided guidance to help those wishing to support participation in decision-making by this group of people. The *See What I Mean* (SWIM) manual suggests that a range of different kinds of information should be used when making inferences about complex and significant choices.

- What is the decision which needs to be made?
- What alternative courses of action are available?
- Is the person aware of the decision that needs to be made?
- Who are the other key people involved?
- What is the range of views among the key people involved in the decision?
- What evidence needs to be collected in order to come to a decision?
- What level of participation in decision-making can be expected from the person?
- What process will you use to reach the decision?

Furthermore, the information needs to be evaluated in terms of how well the person with a learning disability participated in the process of decision-making. The SWIM document provides the following questions as a guide:

- What information do you think the person understood?
- What do you think the person was communicating to you?
- What was the level of his/her participation in the discussion?
- So far as you can tell, was the response
    - typical of the person's usual pattern of communication?
    - better than usual?
    - poorer than usual?
- Was any support provided to help the person communicate?
    - physical prompting?
    - verbal prompting?
    - other?
- Were there any indications that the person was communicating intentionally?

At one level, choosing is so complex that it is a matter for celebration that anyone makes any kind of choice at all. In fact, categorical choices which have a high 'cost', for example, getting married or buying a house, present most people with cause for a great deal of reflection and occasionally anxiety. Other 'everyday choices' are hardly noticed, partly because most of them have a low 'cost' and partly because they can be constantly renegotiated as part of an ongoing process of choosing and rechoosing.

Inviting people to participate in categorical decision-making where the different options have very high costs is much more problematic. As Grove and her colleagues point out, it requires a more systematic method of collecting evidence and a much more cautious approach to inferring both how successfully the person participated in decision-making and to what extent they expressed a preference for one option rather than another.

Privacy versus protection

Effective advocacy depends upon the development of an intimate relationship between the advocate and his or her partner. The better the advocate knows the partner, the more likely it is that he or she will be able to make accurate inferences about likes and dislikes, aspirations and needs. Intimate relationships are usually based upon mutual trust and an appreciation of the boundary between what is private and personal and what can be introduced into a public arena. Most advocacy groups operate an explicit confidentiality policy which formalises the responsibility of the advocate not to reveal information of a personal or private nature.

However, the promotion of intimate and largely private relationships between advocates and their partners is not without risks (see Chapter 8). While partners occasionally choose their own advocate, it is increasingly common for partnerships to be established via advocacy groups, and it is the group which must take responsibility for ensuring that advocates will not take advantage of their privileged position to exploit or abuse their partner. Rigorous selection, screening and induction training are essential, but ongoing monitoring and supervision of advocates is also desirable. There is nevertheless an inherent conflict between promoting intimate and private relationships in order to establish effective advocacy on the one hand, and ensuring that extremely vulnerable people are protected from exploitation and abuse on the other. This dilemma lies at the heart of advocacy and is likely to remain a challenge for the foreseeable future.

Are citizens automatically good advocates?

The term citizen simply refers to a person who lives in a particular country or state and does not in itself imply any particular meritorious qualities. However, it would be naïve to assume that any one inhabitant of a town or county in the UK would make a suitable advocate. As has already been mentioned, effective advocacy depends upon highly sophisticated social skills combined with a high degree of personal integrity. Nevertheless, there is an assumption that advocacy for people who cannot speak up for themselves is best carried out by ordinary people who are untainted by any of the trappings of professionalism.

It might be argued that such ordinary citizens do exist and that the primary task of the advocacy movement is to find out who they are and recruit them as advocates. More realistically, it seems unlikely that many people will already possess the rich combination of personality characteristics, knowledge and skills which make a good advocate and that, as a consequence, varying amounts of induction and 'on the job' training will be beneficial. But does specific training, which is designed to ensure that advocates can perform all their many roles to a high standard, contradict the essential independence and objectivity of the ordinary citizen? There are two answers to this question.
The first is that it very much depends upon the way in which training is provided and the content of a training programme. The second answer is that considering the complexity of the tasks which advocates are expected to address, it would be completely unreasonable and unrealistic to expect anyone to become a citizen advocate *without* extensive training.

Confrontation versus partnership

One of the most common uses of the term 'advocacy' is to describe the role of lawyers in a court of law. UK and North American courts employ an adversarial system which means that the role of the advocate is not to discover the truth of a case, but to convince the jury that one version of events is more plausible than another. As a consequence, advocacy in British and North American courts frequently comes down to opposing and arguing with 'the other side'.

To the extent that one of the roles of a citizen advocate is to ensure that the partners voice is heard by service commissioners and service providers, there is a danger that enthusiastic citizen advocates might be tempted to adopt the adversarial style of courtroom advocates. Similarly, the view that advocacy is part of a political process designed to 'emancipate' or 'empower' an 'oppressed minority' places advocacy in opposition to the establishment as defined by services and government bodies; the relationship of advocates and their partners to services providers and commissioners is reduced to a confrontation between two sides – one powerful and malign representing vested interests, and the other weak and exploited but essentially 'good'.

While legalistic and political metaphors present advocacy as a radical movement with a clear moral purpose, the allusions to confrontation are far from helpful. On the contrary, it might be more productive to view the citizen advocate as an intermediary or arbitrator whose role is to facilitate communication between his or her partner and a variety of other people, some of whom will be service providers or commissioners. It seems likely that such an approach would lead to more effective advocacy, both in terms of improved outcomes for service users and as a way of helping providers and commissioners to deliver high quality services.

The success of advocacy in the longer term will depend upon the breadth of vision it brings to defining and redefining its role. Narrow concepts of advocacy, which see people with a learning disability as locked irretrievably into conflict with those who seek to deny them civil rights and the services to which they are entitled, is likely to restrict opportunities for co-operation and partnership. In contrast, the Scottish Health Advisory Service (SHAS 1998) suggests a number of ways in which partnership with commissioning bodies can help advocacy groups to be more effective. This includes helping advocacy groups to focus on core tasks rather than becoming involved in working groups and consultation exercises; encouraging service providers to support advocacy; encouraging service providers to produce user-friendly information and advice.

SHAS also points out the various ways in which advocacy groups can help commissioners fulfil their responsibilities:

- promoting improvements in health – for example, advocacy provides an extra safeguard to the health and well-being of people who depend upon services
- listening to 'local voices' when assessing needs – for example, individual advocacy can help to put planners in touch with the concerns of individuals
- making the most effective use of resources in commissioning services – for example, advocacy can contribute to a better understanding of a person's needs and so improve the way resources are used
- making sure that providers monitor the quality of their services in promoting high standards – for example, advocacy empowers service users to challenge unacceptable quality of care
- helping people make decisions about their own care and treatment – for example by giving them the time and support they need to arrive at, express and follow though a decision
- helping people move from long-stay hospitals to settings which suit their individual needs and wishes – for example, by ensuring that each individual's unique needs are kept in mind in spite of the urgency of change.

The argument in favour of building partnerships is further developed in respect of funding in the following section.

Funding for advocacy

Limited, often short-term funding has been one of the major factors restricting the growth of advocacy in the UK (Atkinson 1999). Funding from charitable sources has increased considerably with the advent of the National Lottery Charities Board, but like many other charitable funders, NLCB only provides money for fixed term projects. Local advocacy groups, however, depend upon a continuous flow of funds to maintain core administrative activities.

Other potential sources of long-term core funding are the agencies responsible for commissioning learning disability services. However, there are a number of obstacles which need to be overcome. First, commissioning agencies need to be convinced that independent advocacy is an important activity which can lead to significant improvements in the way in which services are developed and provided. Secondly, a local advocacy group will have to demonstrate that it can provide advocacy support of a satisfactory standard. Thirdly, the local group and the commissioning agency will have to establish a method of transferring public funds which protects the independence of advocates and, at the same time, provides the funding agency with assurances in respect of the financial management and probity of the local group.

Achieving the first of these objectives involves raising the profile of advocacy among commissioners and providing evidence of the contribution which effective advocacy can make to service planning and service delivery. Some suggestions about how this might be achieved are described in the previous section. The second objective will require the development of quality assurance procedures, such as voluntary accreditation systems or some form of independent monitoring. Current examples on work in this area include publication by the National Youth Advocacy Service of a set of National Standards (National Youth Advocacy Service, 1999) and the development of an independent advocacy accreditation scheme by a consortium of advocacy groups in Oxfordshire (The Oxfordshire Advocacy Development Group) with the support of local commissioners.

In respect of the third objective, the Scottish Health Advisory Service provides useful guidance for both commissioners and advocacy groups on how to commission advocacy (SHAS 1998). Since the White Paper *Caring for People* specifically excluded advocacy from any contractual arrangements, the SHAS suggests that grant funding is most appropriate. Grants should be based on agreements which set out

- the nature of the activity which is being funded
- the purpose for which the money will be used
- the duration of the agreement
- when the money will be received
- how quality will be monitored
- how disputes will be resolved.

They suggest that monitoring should be carried out as a joint activity. "This means working with agencies to agree the indicators of quality and to agree how evidence can be gathered without damaging the ethos of the project" (SHAS,1998:18).

Summary

There are high expectations about what citizen advocacy can achieve in the future, both for people with severe learning disabilities and complex needs and for those responsible for commissioning and providing services. These expectations will only be met if citizen advocates (individually or as members of groups) recognise the opportunities which exist and adapt to changing circumstances. Advocates need to be equipped with a range of skills so that than can occupy a variety of demanding social roles. Advocacy groups need to establish a collaborative approach so that they can work in partnership not only with people with a learning disability, but also with those responsible for commissioning and providing services.

John Harris

Chief Executive, British Institute of Learning Disabilities

The Projects' Experience
choice through citizen advocacy

One of the five Choice Initiative projects specifically focused on the role of citizen advocacy, while sharing the aim of the other projects in facilitating and maximising choice for people with high support needs. Advocacy was also a recurring theme in the other projects, highlighting the importance of empowerment, autonomy, citizenship and inclusion for people with high support needs, whether through supporting people into mainstream workplaces, enabling them to participate in community activities, offering choice in friendship and leisure, or helping people make choices in the transition to adulthood.

People with high support needs, particularly if they have significant communication difficulties, are dependent on others to advocate for their needs.

> Some participants [in the project] have advocates who support their needs very well, but other participants may not have any relatives, or a keyworker or social worker or anyone to support their needs. In this situation it can be almost impossible for us, as an independent voluntary organisation, to gain their involvement.

The advocacy project

The BILD advocacy project differed from the other four in approaching choice indirectly through focusing on training volunteer advocates rather than hands-on work with people with high support needs. In the citizen advocacy partnership, one person (the 'partner') is at risk of having their choices and decisions ignored through not being heard or listened to. The other person (the 'advocate') seeks to support their partner in representing their wishes and interests. Thus choice and advocacy are strongly linked and the latter can safeguard the former.

The project's original aim was to improve the quality of citizen advocacy by developing training materials which would be prepared and evaluated in consultation with advocacy groups. Consultation resulted in two additional aims: to address recruitment and retention problems by providing materials for initial training and continuing support and development.

The spectrum of advocacy

A striking impression gained from the consultations was the diversity within the citizen advocacy movement. Some groups were closely adhering to the principles of citizen advocacy enumerated by Wolfensberger and O'Brien – sometimes described as 'purist' – which maintained absolute independence and insisted that advocates should receive no rewards in terms of remuneration or academic credits. At the other end of the spectrum were groups which can be described as 'pragmatic'. Some were based in charitable organisations providing contracted-out service, some of which employed paid advocates.

In preparing the *Pathways to Citizen Advocacy* materials, the project sought to reflect this diversity and produce a resource which would represent a balance between different and sometimes conflicting viewpoints.

Is training appropriate?

As the introduction to this chapter pointed out, there is perhaps an assumption that 'ordinary citizens' *can* be citizen advocates, but we cannot assume that everyone who volunteers will already possess the requisite knowledge, skills and personal qualities required to be an effective advocate.

Realistically it seems unlikely that many people will already possess the rich combination of personality characteristics, knowledge and skills needed so varying amounts of induction and 'on the job' training will be beneficial.

The project encountered anecdotal evidence of poor quality advocacy leading to unnecessary difficulties and distress for the advocacy partner. While there are many possible reasons for this, good initial training as well as ongoing support and skill development could help to raise standards.

Some groups – particularly those who sought to adhere strictly to Wolfensberger's model of citizen advocacy (1977, 1983) – were concerned that the training materials might turn advocates into 'mini professionals' who would then be absorbed into the wider service system for people with learning disabilities. This is a legitimate concern which individual advocates and advocacy groups need to bear in mind.

Content of advocacy training

During the initial phase of the project, advocacy groups and partnerships, trainers and others with relevant experience were consulted about the skills and knowledge needed for effective citizen advocacy with people with high support needs.

Communication was consistently the highest priority, particularly in relation to the start of an advocacy partnership and building a relationship with the other person. Two of the seven *Foundation* units focused on communication and a number of the *Advocacy in Context* units looked at issues which the other Choice Initiative projects were tackling.

Pathways to Citizen Advocacy

Foundation Units

- *What Advocacy is About*
- *Disability Awareness and Attitudes*
- *Communication: Getting Started*
- *Communication: Relationship Building*
- *Choices and Decision Making*
- *Conflicts and Complaints*
- *Approaches to Problems.*

Advocacy in Context Units

- *Difference and Diversity*
- *Sexuality*
- *Families, Friends and Volunteers*
- *Working with Professionals*
- *Health and Learning Disabilities*
- *Choice in Where to Live*
- *Choice in Daytime Opportunities*
- *Education and Learning Disabilities*
- *The Law, Learning Disabilities and Citizen Advocacy.*

Delivering advocacy training

Asking volunteers to attend a college course designed for trainee social workers or nurses might well have a detrimental effect. On the other hand, a course designed and delivered specifically for citizen advocates might reasonably be expected to achieve better outcomes. The initial consultation with groups and individuals included discussion about effective methods of training and the resources required.

Piloting the training materials aimed to test out their practicability and usefulness in a variety of settings and ascertain what methods of training were effective. Despite some initial difficulties at the pilot stage, the exercise raised a number of important issues about the delivery of advocacy training. From positive as well as critical feedback it emerged that training materials need to

- allow for flexible planning of sessions
- include handouts for participants
- encourage high levels of engagement and motivation from participants
- use plain language
- have a layout and overall structure which make the materials easy to use.

Advocacy training may be undertaken by the group's own staff or by external trainers, but feedback indicated that groups wanted general advice on how training should be organised, planned and delivered. Allied to this, they emphasised the importance of delivering training, which as far as possible could act as a bridge between training and actual hands-on experience.

The viability of citizen advocacy

The introduction to this chapter has already highlighted some of the difficulties experienced in sustaining advocacy groups – a situation which the project encountered at first hand. One of the groups who had agreed to pilot the training materials dropped out because they had been unable to recruit any volunteers for this. Two groups were on the brink of closure and only saved at the last minute.

Funding was the main problem threatening the viability of advocacy groups. Many had only short-term funding and one-year grants were not uncommon, even from service commissioners. As the project drew to a close, four paid workers in one region had been, or were about to be given, notice because of financial difficulties.

Many groups relied on grants from NHS Trusts or local authorities. National Lottery, charitable bodies and bequests were alternative sources, but were usually time-limited and securing this kind of funding was often largely dependent on luck.

Recruitment and retention of advocates

Even when groups are publicised in the local media, recruitment can be difficult (although there were regional variations):

- citizen advocacy tends to have a low profile locally and nationally
- it is often not considered as an option by potential volunteers
- the long-term commitment required excludes some potential volunteers
- volunteers may not be confident about partnering a person with high support needs.

Suggested strategies to address this included recruiting through local volunteer bureaux and linking up with other groups, including those offering other kinds of advocacy. Both co-ordinators and experienced advocates suggested that more volunteers might be recruited if there were training materials specifically designed for advocates partnering people with high support needs, together with opportunities for meeting potential advocacy partners on a social basis.

Volunteer advocates drop out for a variety of reasons. The project found that

- people who had had a lot of time on their hands could no longer commit the time because, for example, they got a job or a college place
- advocates moved out of the area, perhaps to go to university or because of their partner's employment
- people found the partnerships more demanding and less rewarding than anticipated.

One of the other projects, which had unpaid as well as paid staff (see Chapter 3), faced similar problems and the reasons for drop-out were not dissimilar. They had tried to minimise this by prioritising the training, supervision and support offered – all of which were suggested by advocacy groups too.

Raising the profile of citizen advocacy

Feedback to the project from advocacy groups highlighted the fragmented nature of much of the advocacy movement. Although there were signs of increasing liaison and collaboration which could help raise the profile of citizen advocacy in the future, it sometimes seemed to depend on chance whether an individual was able to access an advocacy service.

> A social worker was extremely concerned that a young woman with high support needs had no one independent of services who could represent her interests as she approached the transition to adulthood. Fortunately he was introduced by the project to a nearby citizen advocacy network (not funded by social services).

> The head of a special school had identified pupils in urgent need of independent advocacy and was guided to the National Youth Advocacy Service. In both instances we may ask: 'why didn't they know about these resources themselves?'

However, even when an advocacy partnership had been set up, lack of official recognition could create significant obstacles.

The project heard a number of accounts where citizen advocates were denied access to residential homes or day centres, or refused information relating to major concerns about their partner. There were also instances of advocates being ignored by service commissioners or providers – or even told outright that as advocates they had no standing.

From this and the other projects, it is clear that there are many individuals with high support needs for whom powerful advocacy could be a means of greater empowerment and choice-making in their lives, but with the current vulnerable fragmentary service which lacks adequate recognition, this will be difficult to achieve.

Cheryl, *a young woman who had lived in institutions since the age of eight, was thought to have little or no ability to communicate verbally. Cheryl acquired an advocate and, after many months building a good relationship with her, the advocate discovered that she could speak quite well, but because her responses tended to be delayed by about ten seconds her voice always went unheard. Cheryl and her advocate agreed that Cheryl would hold the advocate's elbow and when she wanted to speak would give it a gentle squeeze. The advocate would then stop talking until Cheryl had had her say. This was so successful that her carers adopted it, and so Cheryl began to find her voice. This led to a number of changes in her life including a move from day centre to college, a reduction in her medication, and attempts being made to find her family with whom she had completely lost contact.*

Denise *has always used sign language. Though unable to speak, signing had enabled her to communicate very effectively and she had helped care staff improve their signing. However, as she grew older, Denise developed arthritis in her hands which affected her ability to sign clearly. Partly because of the distress this caused her, Denise was offered a citizen advocate, although in the early days of their partnership the advocate was unable to sign and had to use a textbook when communicating with Denise. She coped with the advocate's lack of knowledge by pointing to diagrams of signs in the book. For Denise this became a new and effective way of communicating.*

Atkinson. D. (1999) *Advocacy: A Review.* Unpublished report prepared for the Joseph Rowntree Foundation.

British Institute of Learning Disabilities (2000) *Pathways To Citizen Advocacy.* Kidderminster: BILD.

Grove, N. (in press) *See What I Mean: Guidelines to Aid Understanding of Communication by People with Severe and Profound Learning Disabilities.* Kidderminster: BILD Publications.

Grove, N., Porter, J., Bunning, K. and Olsson, C. (1999) *Interpreting the meaning of communication by people with severe and profound intellectual disabilities: theoretical and methodological issues.* Journal of Applied Research in Intellectual Disabilities, 12, 3: 190-203.

Hewett, D. and Nind, M. (1998) *Interaction in Action: Reflections on the Use of Intensive Interaction.* London. David Fulton.

Lord Chancellor's Department, (1997) *Who Decides? Making Decisions on Behalf of Mentally Incapacitated Adults.* Cm 3803. London: The Stationery Office

Lord Chancellor's Department, (1999) *Making Decisions: The Government's Proposals for Making Decisions on Behalf of Mentally Incapacitated Adults.* Cm 4465. London: The Stationery Office.

National Youth Advocacy Service (1999) *National Standards for Agencies Providing Advocacy for Children and Young People.* Wirral: NYAS

Nind, M. and Hewett, D. (1994) *Access to Communication: Developing the Basics of Communication with People with Severe Learning Difficulties Through Intensive Interaction.* London: David Fulton.

Scottish Health Advisory Service and Scottish Office (1998) *Advocacy: A Guide to Good Practice.* Dd 8457633, 10/98. London: The Stationery Office.

Wolfensberger, W. (1977) *A Balanced Multi-Component Advocacy/Protection Scheme.* Toronto: Canadian Association for the Mentally Retarded.

Wolfensberger, W. (1983) *Reflections on the Status of Citizen Advocacy.* Toronto: National Institute of Mental Retardation.

Wood, D., Bruner, J.S. and Ross, G. (1976) *The role of tutoring in problem solving.* Journal of Child Psychology and Psychiatry, 17, 2:89-100.

Wood, H.A. and Wood, D.J. (1984) *An experimental evaluation of the effects of five styles of teacher conversation on the language of hearing impaired children.* Journal of Child Psychology and Psychiatry, 25, 1:45 –62.

Risk
and choice

INTRODUCTION

This introduction examines the tensions between empowerment and protection in the development of support for people with learning disabilities. We move from the concern with dangerousness and protection that underpinned the development of institutions and consider how the subsequent reaction against excessive protection was associated with an emphasis on empowering people with learning disabilities. We then look at the current tensions between empowerment and protection and examine how these tensions can be creatively managed.

From protection to empowerment

In the 1960s, there was growing public awareness that institutions were causing harm. The response was a commitment to empowerment, and in particular to enabling individuals with learning disabilities to experience ordinary living. This commitment underpinned the influential King's Fund's *Ordinary Life* initiative.

> Mentally handicapped people have the same rights and, as far as possible, the same responsibilities as all other members of the community... Those who serve mentally handicapped people have a duty to ensure that opportunities to live life to the full are available to them. *(King's Fund, 1980: 14)*

The Jay Committee Report on *Mental Handicap Nursing and Care* also accepted the importance of empowerment through ordinary life experiences, arguing that a balance between empowerment and protection could and should be created through the development of risk management policies.

> The question of risk is one of extreme delicacy for those who care. Staff are likely to receive harsh criticism when accident or injury occurs, yet if we entirely cushion people against these dangers we immediately restrict their lives and their chances of development. This restriction can be cloaked in respectability and defended on the grounds of protecting mentally handicapped people and keeping them safe, but it can also endanger human dignity. Each of us lives in a world which is not always safe, secure and predictable; mentally handicapped people too need to assume a fair and prudent share of risk... each [residential] unit should have a well defined policy on risk-taking... we do not want mentally handicapped people to be completely insulated from the day-to-day risks to which everybody else is exposed, but the balance between acceptable risk-taking and irresponsibility on the part of residential care staff is a delicate one, which varies from case to case. *(Jay Committee, 1979: paras. 121, 308)*

The tension between empowerment and protection

Despite the Jay Committee's recommendations, there is little evidence that service agencies have developed effective strategies to balance empowerment and protection. Nearly two decades later the Social Services Inspectorate noted that

> in some cases, although staff may have undertaken a risk assessment prior to supporting people in new activities, case files did not record these assessments and decision. Within Social Services Departments, we found it difficult to determine a consistent line to risk-taking issues, particularly where these were not well documented. Even where they existed, not all staff, nor users and carers, were aware of written guidelines on risk-taking. *(Fruin, 1998: para 6.6.)*

Failure to develop effective policies and practices for risk is beginning to undermine the progress made in the last 30 years. The benefits of care within the community and of the empowerment of vulnerable individuals are being questioned. Some relatives and carers believe that agencies do not provide adequate protection and concerns are being expressed about the way agencies respond to harmful behaviours.

Concerns about abuse

There is some evidence that families do not feel that their vulnerable relatives are getting adequate protection and are at risk of abuse. This has led some to campaign for a return to more protected and secure environments typified by the 'village community' movement.

Concerns about vulnerability have also attracted academic attention, especially in debates about abuse. Brown, for example, provides

> an overview of abuse as an issue in the lives of people with learning disabilities, and of 'adult protection' as a role in, and for, service agencies... It would seem that people with learning disabilities have always been at risk in services, in their families and in wider communities, so it is important to maintain a critical stance towards the current heightened concern about their vulnerability and questions why it has emerged at this time. *(Brown, 1999: 89)*

Vulnerability and dangerousness

Developing effective services for vulnerable individuals has proved difficult. With an increasingly vociferous mass media, any serious accident or incident is likely to attract considerable attention and the agency involved can expect to be blamed for failing to protect the individuals who were harmed.

High profile incidents concerning individuals with serious mental illness have generated a moral panic and have been used as 'evidence' that the 'liberal' policy of community care with its emphasis on empowering vulnerable people has failed.

High profile incidents involving people with learning disabilities have generally been ones in which the individuals themselves have been harmed. Two incidents in 1998, for example, resulted in the accidental deaths of individuals participating in leisure activities. Barry Denne was on a holiday in Majorca organised by his residential care home when he went missing and was found dead (*Guardian,* 1998a, 5). John McGill, Beverly Wilson, Peter Burgess and Eric Jones died in an accident on a canal holiday organised by their day centre. Canal trips are a common activity at this centre and this group has been on holiday together before. They had been active members of the local community, taking part in many of the ordinary community events and involved in education, health and employment schemes in Barrow (*Guardian,* 1998b, 10).

Risk and empowerment: current policies and practice

In 1998 we undertook a survey of risk assessment and management, and how agencies sought to balance safety and empowerment (Alaszewski et al, 1999). Thirty-one agencies participated, including statutory, voluntary and private providers.

All agencies accepted that safety was a prime objective for organisations providing support for people with learning disabilities. Agencies in the independent sector are required to meet the demands of the statutory sector in order to gain registration and pass inspections.

Most agencies identified health and safety policies as the main mechanism for ensuring safety but reported that other policies were also in place to ensure users' safety, including individual life plans or care plans. These plans were based on an assessment of the client which identified any potential risks for the individual, and the steps taken to manage the risk.

The majority of managers also acknowledged the importance of empowering service users and our analysis of their comments identified three interlinked elements of empowerment strategies.

- **Philosophies** or value bases which emphasised the importance of user empowerment. A third of respondents stated that their general service policies were developed using an explicit philosophy or set of values based on the work of either Wolfensberger or O'Brien's five principles of service development.
- **Policies** which provided an empowerment framework for practice and decision-making. A number of agencies had explicit policies designed to support and empower the users of their services. Some agencies had polices which empowered service users by providing them with opportunities for participation in agency decisions, such as in recruitment and selection procedures.
- **Procedures** designed to ensure that user empowerment informed agency practices and the ways in which it is carried out. Most agencies had key workers who were expected to represent the interests of specific users.

However when we explored the relationship between safety and empowerment, especially in risk issues, we found that concerns with safety tended to override the desire to empower users. This bias towards safety was evident in their definitions of risk, location of risk policies and attitudes towards staff implicit within policies.

Respondents tended to define risk negatively, as a hazard or harm to clients. Only a minority saw risk in terms of empowerment or opportunity, or as a balance between safety and empowerment.

This bias towards safety was reflected in the fact that the issue of risk was usually addressed within health and safety policies with the emphasis on hazards which can harm staff and users, and which can be identified and measured using a checklist. We found few specific risk policies which were explicitly designed to bridge the protection/empowerment divide and which recognised that protection and empowerment needed to be negotiated and agreed.

The bias towards safety was also reflected in agencies' attitudes towards their staff. Despite claims that they tried to avoid a 'blaming' culture, most managers described systems which emphasised a safety culture. Designed to ensure that staff were clearly aware of their responsibilities, there was usually a clear procedure for taking action if anything went wrong. The overwhelming majority of agencies had clear structures of accountability, usually involving job descriptions, line management and regular supervision with disciplinary codes and provision for formal investigation of incidents.

This contrasted with an approach based on trust in staff, with an emphasis on learning from incidents encouraging staff to share information. A minority of managers felt their agency did provide a mechanism for staff to obtain feedback, through supervision, meetings, debriefing sessions and discussions. However, although most respondents claimed that staff would be offered protection if they reported incidents, it was clear that this would be overridden by the agency's need to investigate.

What emerges clearly from our survey, is that agencies are concerned about safety and empowerment but in practice safety issues tend to dominate. They saw this partly as a response to external pressures, including

- legislation, particularly health and safety requirements
- joint commissioning between health and social service departments, quality audits and multi-agency work
- a culture of suing and litigation
- concern about adverse media coverage.

Getting the balance right

As we enter the 21st century, agencies and individuals supporting individuals with learning disabilities need to find ways of creating and sustaining a realistic balance between empowerment and protection that avoids laissez-faire optimism on the one hand, and the repressive pessimism that permeated institutions on the other. We believe that this balance can be achieved by taking on board the following issues.

Commitment to the interests of people with learning disabilities

Empowerment is often seen as indicating a commitment to the interests of people with learning disabilities. However, empowerment which exposes individuals to unreasonable risks is clearly *not* in their interests. Their interests are best served by 'reasonable' or acceptable risk-taking in which there is a balance of potential opportunities and benefits provided by risk-taking against the possible harms. As Tindall has pointed out such an approach would

> provide a clear, systematic and focused way of assisting people with learning difficulties to take risks which genuinely lead to more control over their lives.
> *(Tindall, 1997: 117)*

Openness and a willingness to admit and learn from errors

The best way of building confidence in the community and minimising unfounded fears is to have policies which provide an assurance that the agency and its employees have a clear awareness of hazards and risk issues, as well as decision-making processes which enable them to balance reasonable risk-taking with safety and protection of users, staff and the public.

Despite people's best intentions and even working within a clear policy framework, accidents will happen resulting in harm to individuals with a learning disability. However, the existence of a clear policy and evidence that all individuals have acted within this framework would enable agencies and professionals to justify their actions (Tindall, 1997: 117). Openness in such circumstances is essential and lessons learned.

Sincerity and trust

Abuse in institutions has probably done much to undermine the confidence of carers and others in services. In the past relatives were assured that the professionals who were assuming responsibility for their relative would ensure their safety and protection and minimise harm. This confidence was sometimes misplaced and trust betrayed. If a new relationship of trust is to be created then it is important that carers and others believe that individuals providing care and support are sincere and trustworthy.

Trust is an elusive concept and how it develops is unclear, but it seems to have something to do with sincerity – the extent to which people believe the agency and its staff are honest (eg Metlay, 1999: 102). This integrity can be demonstrated by shared respect and understanding of individuals with learning disabilities and reinforced by a willingness to communicate and share information with all those involved in care and support.

Andy Alaszewski

Professor of Health Studies, University of Hull

Helen Alaszewski

Researcher, Community and Health Studies, University of Hull

The Projects' Experience
risk and choice

Risk and empowerment are inter-related, and as the Choice Initiative's main aim was to enable people with high support needs to exercise more choice in their lives, risk was a live issue for all the projects. Although, as the introduction to this chapter pointed out, there has been a shift away from an overprotective stance towards people with learning disabilities and greater emphasis on empowerment, individuals with high support needs may continue to be seen as more vulnerable and more in need of protection. As the handbook produced by the *Pathways to Citizen Advocacy* project pointed out

> choice for all of us involves trying things out, making mistakes, changing our minds and a process of trial and error. It is often assumed that people with severe learning disabilities need to be protected from these things, where in fact the support they require is in experiencing them.

The issue of risk touched all the different stakeholders in the Choice Initiative, albeit in different ways. Project managers and staff sometimes felt they were taking huge risks in supporting people out in the community and in the workplace. The participants themselves were risking new experiences, going to new places and making new relationships. Family carers were understandably concerned about safety and whether their relative was being set up to fail. Service providers were being asked to work together with newly established projects.

Some participants seemed to feel more confident and comfortable in new situations and better able to handle change than others, but one of the successes of the Choice Initiative was undoubtedly its positive impact on the lives of some individuals.

Thinking about risk

The Foundation's workshop on choice for people with high support needs was led by Michelle Cuffe and Dave Helm from United Response. The event included an exploration of risk to help projects work positively with this issue. Participants were asked to think about a scenario, which raised the question of how to balance choice with the duty to care and then to look at situations in their own organisations.

They were reminded that risk assessment is a tool to enable us and those we support to benefit from new opportunities and remain as safe as possible. This is achieved by
- recognising rights
- recognising risks
- minimising risks
- reaching consensus/negotiating together
- recording clearly
- reviewing regularly.

What is risk?

1. If you are alive, you will from time to time be in a situation which puts you at risk.

2. Risks are therefore unavoidable from time to time.

3. Having a learning disability can give rise to added risks because of misunderstandings; lack of awareness of danger; communication difficulties; associated difficulties, such as loss of sight or hearing; other health problems such as epilepsy.

4. Managing risks thus becomes crucial in fulfilling our duty to care and promoting choice.

What kinds of risks?

The issue of risk and people with learning disabilities is often dominated by considerations of physical safety. Important though these are, the projects found that other elements need to be recognised too – the risk of going into new situations (however physically safe they might be); the risk of allowing oneself to communicate with another person and becoming vulnerable; the risk of making relationships; the risk that life will change and will it be for the better?

Risk and relationships

Each participant in a project was risking 'getting to know' a new person in their life and this relationship building was sometimes difficult when that person felt unsure.

> Andrew was clearly unsure about the [employment project] and we had to take time in our relationships with him, allowing him to make choices and me to listen and understand him.

> Because Peter wanted to work, it was important for us to build a relationship concentrating on respect for each other, setting boundaries and discussing consequences of his behaviour.

Projects found a number of ways to address this issue, including establishing ways of communicating with one another; allowing time for people to get to know one another; always going at the participant's pace; building trust and confidence; spending time with people in familiar situations where they felt safe; and sometimes initially working alongside a person they already knew.

The Friendship Train aimed to facilitate friendships among people with high support needs, but this can be risky.

> Friendship can lead to new demands and problems – abuse, intimacy, relationships which don't fit into services, and so on.

Informed risk

Risk assessment includes being aware of potential risks. All projects recognised the importance of involving 'third parties' from the start, including addressing concerns about risk expressed by family members or care staff. But these other people were also crucial informants, helping project staff build a fuller picture of an individual including situations which might place someone at risk, whether this was lifting and handling someone in the right way; or knowing that certain situations might make someone scream or cause them to try and run away.

The Communication Passport (see Chapter 2) can be another way of understanding and recording risk for an individual. A passport for someone with physical disabilities, for example, might include the following information:

- I need two or three people to lift me and I really should have a hoist to help me feel safe and secure
- I need to get a proper risk assessment for moving and handling; I don't want to be dropped or to fall, or for anyone to hurt themselves
- I would always like to be supported at mealtimes by people who know me well, otherwise I may not eat properly
- I spend a lot of time in my wheelchair, which can cause pressure sores, I need to get out of my chair every hour to lie on the floor, or sit in my comfortable armchair at home.

Occasionally project workers also found it useful to consult professionals. Speech therapists could sometimes help with communication issues. For example, Paul has Tourette's Syndrome and his project worker talked to a speech therapist about possible strategies to help him communicate more effectively with Paul and help him understand Paul's ways of communicating.

Risking new experiences

Most people find the idea of change difficult. Even when chosen rather than imposed, it can still feel daunting. Often something new can feel exciting *and* frightening.

> Paul was saying, "I am ready [for work]" and then screaming.

> Andrew's first few weeks at work were a risky business and I believe he was terrified of failing.

Projects were acknowledging people's rights to participate in mainstream employment and community activities, often for the first time. Staff minimised the risks through a combination of practical and emotional support.

For example, the supported employment project
- explained that everyone was worried when they started a new job
- provided constant reassurance
- gave people as much information as possible
- organised pre-placement visits to the workplace
- encouraged people to share their worries at the Job Club
- ensured that people's support circles were kept informed and provided additional encouragement.

The project supporting people to use mainstream community facilities found that people would try out new activities.

> But they needed time to become familiar with new experiences and places. New experiences needed to be introduced, repeated, explored and developed but, crucially, at the participant's pace and in their own way.

For the employment project, it was perhaps more risky. Participants were being expected to do a job, with all the responsibility for accomplishing specific tasks that that entailed. Andrew, who found it difficult to understand what 'employment' meant in practice, could only find out through experience.

> At first he found it quite difficult because he didn't know what was happening to him, so he actually got physically ill and he didn't want to go to work. But after a few times... he was just a changed person; he began to learn his job and know his routines.

Risk in the workplace

The job search and job analysis elements of supported employment involved an appraisal of possible risks and devising strategies to minimise these.

> Although a likeable man, Peter could be quite stubborn and his mischievous nature sometimes meant he was sometimes rather overly energetic. His job trainer worked with him on a set of ground rules so that he would understand how he would be expected to behave at work. Although Peter has limited verbal communication, he can list the rules which are to walk quietly through the store, and walk and move around slowly. These have minimised the risk of Peter losing his placement because of his behaviour, but have also enabled him to become more independent in the workplace.

Risk in the community

People with high support needs are often isolated from their community. Sometimes this is because there are physical barriers, but often it is because there are insufficient resources to ensure adequate support. The Choices project always worked with a ratio of two-to-one which minimised possible risk. As one participant's residential support worker reported

> the project allows him to do community-based activities which require 2:1 staffing, which cannot always be supplied from [our] residential staff team. It allows safety and reassurance in trying new activities, building confidence and self-esteem.

People living with family carers often faced similar obstacles as parents, particularly if they were elderly, did not always feel confident about accompanying their son or daughter into the community. This was one of the difficulties which the Friendship Train encountered and led them to working directly with the individual, rather than trying to involve their immediate carer. However, this had its own attendant risks, particularly when people no longer met at the project base, but started meeting in ordinary community facilities.

The Choices project successfully involved a volunteer with a mild learning disability by ensuring that both he and the person he worked with were well supported.

> G is a volunteer with a mild learning disability who has been working with Nicos in the Sensory Session. The two men had established a good relationship and G was enthusiastic about doing more independent activities with Nicos. A was recruited as a new worker to support G on Choices and together, they spent a couple of weeks at a day centre Nicos uses to learn how to support him while swimming. G and A are now working from Nicos' home to access his local area. Meanwhile, a second support worker was brought in for a few weeks to ensure things are safe and that G is confident about his new role.

Opening emotional doors

Encouraging people to communicate and reach out to others could, as a project manager said, "bring up deep hurt or absolute joy". For some individuals, their involvement in the Choice Initiative had many positive outcomes which went beyond the immediate focus of the project so the risks were worthwhile. Susan's participation resulted in a successful work placement but there were other benefits.

> Susan has blossomed. She feels more valued and she has started to emerge from her often withdrawn state, she reaches out more to other people and has developed some good relationships with people her own age.

Not everyone responded in this way, however, and sometimes the consequences of risking new activities and situations were less positive. Despite considerable initial anxieties, Paul settled into a work placement and was getting on well with his support worker and his colleagues in the factory, but then things began to change.

> Paul's formerly good relationship with his support worker seemed to hit a bad patch. He was also increasingly anxious to get in touch with his father [with whom he'd had no contact for a long time]. Eventually he refused to go to work, became extremely aggressive but was also very depressed. No one in the project is certain about what triggered this situation, but after some months, although Paul is still very emotional, he seems to be emerging from his sadness and is saying that he is ready to work again.

> Having apparently settled in well at the sports centre and enjoying it, after a few months, Andrew refused to continue with the work placement. He became more and more angry and aggressive with everyone. This has been a difficult experience for Andrew and those who support him, including his mum. Project staff are still trying to understand what might have triggered Andrew's very angry feelings and have continued to be involved with him and his mum, even though Andrew is no longer part of the project.

Recognising that the project was opening 'emotional doors' for some people, project staff developed strategies which could begin to address these unanticipated situations. These included

- creating time and space to listen to the person and trying to understand their difficulties
- talking to the person's support circle, family members, etc, and drawing on their knowledge and support
- initiating referrals to people, such as counsellors, psychologists or social workers who might help with advice on communication or behaviour and support the individual
- ensuring that the workers were supported.

By offering participants the possibility of making choices and exercising greater control over their lives, the Choice Initiative hoped to improve individuals' quality of life and general well-being. For the majority of people this proved to be the case. For others, the psychological impact of participating in the project pointed to a need for help in addressing these issues. Adults with high support needs, accustomed to being dependent, may want this to change, but at the same time they may find the prospect too daunting. They may experience conflicting feelings about independence, feel too vulnerable to risk new experiences, and lack a strong enough sense of self to deal with new challenges.

Conclusion

This chapter has generally focused on how risk affected individual participants and the strategies which projects used to address this. However, as briefly mentioned at the start, project staff could also feel they were at risk in supporting people to make choices which might be risky. Good management and regular support and supervision were essential if staff themselves were to feel confident about their work and these issues are discussed in the following chapter.

Alaszewski, A., Alaszewski, H. and Parker, A. (1999) *Empowerment and Protection*. London: Mental Health Foundation.

Brown, H. *Abuse of People with Learning Disabilities: Layers of Concern and Analysis* in Stanley, N., Manthorpe, J. and Penhale, B. *Institutional Abuse: Perspectives Across the Life Course*. Routledge, London.

Fruin, D. (1998) *Moving into Mainstream: The Report of a National Inspection of Services for Adults with Learning Disabilities*. London: Department of Health.

Guardian (1998a), *Handicapped man lost in Majorca*, 29 September 1998, p5.

Guardian (1998b), *Care Centre grieves as victims of narrow boat accident named*, 21 August 1998, p10.

Jay, P. (1979) *Report of the Committee of Enquiry into Mental Handicap Nursing and Care*, London: HMSO.

King's Fund (1980) *An Ordinary Life: Comprehensive Locally-based Residential Services for Mentally Handicapped People*, Project Paper, no 24. London: King's Fund.

Metlay, D. (1999) *Institutional Trust and Confidence: A Journey into a Conceptual Quagmire* in Cvetkovich, G. and Löfstedt, R. E. (eds) *Social Trust and the Management of Risk*. London: Earthscan.

Tindall, B. (1997) *People with Learning Difficulties: Citizenship, Personal Development and the Management of Risk* in Kemshall, H. and Pritchard, J. (eds) *Good Practice in Risk Assessment and Risk Management 2, Protection, Rights and Responsibilities*. London: Jessica Kingsley Publishers.

Staff
development and training

INTRODUCTION

For as long as I have worked in the social care sector, there has been a move away from the idea that "the professionals know best". Looking back over 17 years, I am struck by the increasing simplicity of the language and content used in a wide variety of course materials. I equate simplicity with depth and this has always led me to be suspicious of anything, anyone or any movement that seeks to make simple things complicated. Take, for example, the Open University Course *Equal People* (Open University, 1996). The title says it all. The course materials are easy to read, challenging to discuss and difficult to put into practice. Easy to read, because the authors want all sorts of people to join in the course; people with a learning disability, friends, families and professionals. Challenging to discuss, because there is still so much to do to make our communities more naturally welcoming and inclusive. Difficult to put into practice, because there are no formulae, no blueprints and no professionals who know best.

A new professionalism?

In effect, a new kind of professionalism is emerging, based on a family of values, assumptions and activities that seek to put the person with a learning disability at the centre of every decision. Person-centred planning (see also Chapters 3 and 5) challenges professionals (and some parents who may find it difficult to see their sons and daughters as grown-up) to consider the balance of power in their relationships. We are engaged in the business of learning how to change from having 'power over' people to having 'power with' people. These are not just ideas.

The principle of partnership with service users, carers and professionals is built into UK legislation. The development of the Department of Health's new strategy for learning disability services is based on consulting with people with a learning disability, as well as with their carers and with professionals. Sub-groups are working on health, children, independence, workforce planning, carers, and building partnerships. It is clear from this list that the Department of Health has attempted to bridge the social care/health care divide that has characterised so much of the training offered to people drawn to work alongside people with a learning disability.

Work on developing the strategy focuses on the whole person, and assumes that individuals will be included in the worlds of education, employment, leisure and healthy lifestyles. The Department of Health intends to play its part in ensuring that health and social services staff of all persuasions work together to serve the best interests of those using their services. This suggests that person-centred planning is beginning to be addressed at the strategic level.

Modernising services

Modernisation is one of the government's catchphrases. The Department of Health's recent publication, *Modernising Social Services* (Department of Health, 1998) states

> our proposals will modernise social services. We will work with local government and others to make sure that our objectives and specific targets are met, and real improvements achieved.

The document goes on to spell out some of the ways in which this will happen and the kind of differences it will make to people's lives.

> Services will promote and enhance people's independence, with better prevention an rehabilitation services established with the help of the additional funding the government is providing; and many more people will use direct payments schemes to have real control over how their care needs are provided for.

> Services will meet each individual's needs, with social services providing an integrated service with the NHS and other agencies, pooling budgets where appropriate.

> Everyone will be safeguarded against abuse, neglect, or poor treatment while receiving care. Standards will be clearer, checks will be tighter and the Commission for Care Standards will have strong and swift powers to put a stop to any abuse where it occurs.

> Social care staff will have clearer standards and better training arrangements, overseen by the General Social Care Council. Our targets for improving training levels will mean that people will benefit from safe, skilled and competent care staff.

> People will be able to have confidence in dependable local social services, knowing that through the Best Value regime, checks are made both locally and nationally to ensure that services are to scratch, and action will be taken if standards are not to be met.

These are an impressive set of objectives. However, they are only likely to be achieved if the skills, values and knowledge inherent in effective person-centred planning are embedded in every training initiative. Person-centred planning approaches – which start with the person and then move on to developing ways of addressing their needs – are as useful to GPs and other primary care team members as they are to day care workers. They have as much to offer consultant psychiatrists as they do factory workers. Person-centred approaches seek to embrace the important aspects of life – emotional, spiritual, physical realities – that describe a person in rich detail.

Implications for future training

I have recently been part of a team writing training materials for a Diploma in Supported Employment (Open Training College, Dublin, 1998). However, there are, as yet, no Diploma courses in Supported Living, Supported Education or Supported Leisure. When and if these training courses emerge, they must offer a consistent and unified person-centred approach, otherwise there is a danger that we will perpetuate diverse and separate specialisms with professional cultures to match. Future training will need to address the different domains in people's *lives* but avoid recreating rigid service demarcations of residential and day services.

The starting-point for future training initiative must be the needs of people with learning disabilities. The Diploma has been a case in point. It emerged because supported employment practitioners had developed a body of knowledge and a battery of skills through supporting individuals into paid work, but were keen to get better at delivering that support.

Limitations of training?

Although new training initiatives can equip staff with the knowledge and skills to support people in more inclusive settings, it is also important to recognise the limitations of training, particularly in relation to attitudes or values. A local authority may decide to replace its traditional five-days-a-week, buildings-based day service with a more flexible support service, operating seven days a week, because that is what service users want. Training may then address issues such as supporting people in community settings or in their own homes, but if staff are opposed to these changes, there are limits to what any training programme will achieve. *Can* it tackle these attitudinal barriers?

Radical changes in services such as those described above will run out of steam if the lessons from person-centred planning and the growing movement for inclusion are not built into the way we think about training. We need people who know how to commission person-centred services but, even more importantly, we need people with a solid skills base which can equip them to work alongside people with learning disabilities and enable them to achieve the goals of their individual person-centred plans. Purchasing and commissioning person-centred support services will not suffice.

As you read through the stories and experiences in the rest of this chapter, you will see how things begin to change when parents, carers, friends, staff and advocates in the various projects worked through their own version of developing 'power with' rather than 'power over' people with a learning disability.

Tony Phillips

Director of the Realife Trust

The Projects' Experience
staff development and training

When setting up the Choice Initiative, the Foundation recognised the importance of skilling and supporting the project staff who would be working in what often turned out to be ground-breaking and challenging work with people with high support needs. By running a series of workshops, and facilitating regular opportunities for project staff to meet and discuss their work with one another, the Foundation's input was an important addition to the training and development activities within the projects themselves.

> Meeting with people from the other projects was good. We were all finding it hard and discovering this early on was good. I also felt we were able to be quite honest with [the Foundation] about this.

> I think the meetings have given us all the chance to talk about what we've been doing... you can check out what you're doing and listen to other people and see whether their work is going along the same lines and whether they are having the same problems.

As Tony Phillips pointed out in the introduction to this chapter, "a new kind of professionalism is emerging" which encompasses values and attitudes as well as skills but, above all, places the person with a learning disability at the centre.

> We have offered [support] from trustworthy capable staff (paid and voluntary) who we believe have what it takes (though the 'what' is hard to analyse) to really put the clients' interests first and be responsible for empowering clients at all times.

Personal qualities and attitudes

The projects recruited a range of paid (and in the case of one project, also volunteer) staff from different backgrounds. Some people were appointed who had relevant skills and/or experience; the Friendship Train workers, for example, were both experienced group facilitators and had previously worked with people with high support needs and communication difficulties. What became clear, however, was that the personal attitudes and qualities people brought to the work were of paramount importance as the Markfield Project found.

> Staff recruitment was difficult... I searched among our pool of sessional workers for people who were of the same gender, ethnic background and age... It became clear that it was neither possible nor necessary to fulfil all these criteria in all cases. The fundamental skills and attitudes of the staff became most important. Those who responded well to clients and had a respect and enthusiasm for the aims of the project were the most successful at building relationships and accessing activities.

During the lifetime of the projects, it became clear that staff needed some specific skills and qualities to empower people and enable them to make choices. This was important in terms of recruitment but also emphasised the importance of supervision and training where these could be developed and worked on.

As Chapter 2 has suggested, *listening* to someone, *observing* them and *being responsive* to them were all pre-requisites for understanding an individual and their communications, and building a relationship with them. Projects found that these listening skills could be learned and practised but, to varying degrees, they were skills we already use in personal relationships: "those peripheral, intangible qualities such as intuition, empathy..." What was important was

> being there and being ourselves... [but also] finding ways of entering the other person's world and letting them know that you understand.

What emerged from all the projects was something hard to define but basically about using oneself; it was often the worker's own feelings and reactions which helped them understand and relate to participants – qualities which might be described as empathy, intuition, perception. Project staff also spoke of the need to respect and acceptance of the person being supported. Participants needed people "who would be non-judgemental and who would express pleasure and interest in what they did and how they were". It also meant respecting the way people communicated.

> You have to have a certain honesty... You are challenged to look within yourself and see whether how you are interpreting somebody's way of communicating is really honest and true.

Respect for people's choices is a central plank of the citizen advocacy role and BILD's training materials explored this issue in some detail. For the other projects too, this need to respect people's choices was fundamental. Staff had to focus continually on the other person's needs and not their own agenda.

> If you are offering options to a participant, you must be careful to include things which you don't like personally but which the participant may enjoy, eg types of music, sugar in your tea, walking in the rain. It's almost too easy to influence the activities that you undertake. It is vital that staff look for signals from the participants and develop **their interests.**

As other chapters have already recounted, respecting a person's choice could sometimes be very challenging. When a Step Out participant chose not to continue with a work placement, for example, this was not only difficult for their supported employment worker but was something which the whole project had to face. If your mission is to support people into work, it isn't easy when someone makes it clear that this is not their choice.

In most services, people with high support needs have little if any choice about who provides their support. Although the projects could not always offer participants unlimited choice, they were attempting to respect individual choice in this matter.

Everyone is likely to be drawn towards some people and to find others less to their liking, but respecting individual choice meant that project staff sometimes had to face rejection in the relationship whilst maintaining their self-confidence and commitment to the project – and their hopes for that person. Sometimes it was a temporary or momentary rejection when staff had to accept that support could mean standing back and respecting a person's wish to be alone:

> Many people would be offended by being pushed away, but G was delighted when Andreas became assertive enough that he pushed him off the sofa. G took this as a communication that he wanted to be alone and he respected this.

Neither of these scenarios is particularly unusual. Indeed they will be familiar to anyone employed in a service setting. What marks these encounters is the fact that project workers were focusing on the underlying communication – not seeing it as 'challenging behaviour' or 'being difficult' – and were responding accordingly.

Project workers needed *self-confidence*, particularly when out and about in the community with participants. This was something which could be developed and sustained through regular support and supervision but needed to be there, in some measure, from the start.

> I've learned about my own confidence in working with people in public... and how much support you need to start with... to actually go out with someone, particularly if they have an obvious physical disability, you've got to cope with other people's reactions as much as with the person you're working with... that's been quite an interesting insight. It does take some special people to stand up and say that their client is a person who lives in the community and has every right to be included in **their** shopping centre.

Moving on from there, enabling a participant to begin making relationships with other people also required self-confidence. Explaining to a shop assistant how someone communicates other than with words, asking them to watch out for you next time you visit, and doing this in a way which was unpatronising and avoided 'speaking for them' was not easy.

At one of the Foundation's meetings, project staff talked of the importance of participants being "allowed to make mistakes" and try again. This was not surprising, given that the projects were involved in exploring and trying out new ways of responding to individuals. Staff mentioned the need to be *imaginative and creative* as well as *flexible and adaptive,* both in terms of the overall project but also with individuals. *Problem-solving* approaches and what is sometimes described as a *'can do'* attitude were often important in moving forward; as someone said at one of the Foundation's project meetings: "Nothing is carved in stone".

> Developing a long-term structure which explores the daily lives and long-term hopes and dreams of a group of young people [with high support needs] has involved many rethinks and a few abandoned ideas along the way.

Capturing the learning by making time for *reflection* can be difficult in action research projects of this kind, although reports to the Foundation and regular meetings hosted by the Foundation provided some structured opportunities.

In the Choices project, staff completed a form after each session which asked them to think about the session from the individual's perspective as well as their own by asking the following questions:

For the **individual:**
How was it? What were the significant moments? Would you like to do anything from today again?

For the **worker:**
How did you work with your client? What were the significant moments? How did you feel about your work today?

From these forms, they have been able to reflect on what the users' needs are and also those of the staff.

Keeping going: support and supervision

> The work is very demanding... it is also rewarding but people do lose energy... the people that are actually providing the support need to be motivated; that's a big factor; it's a major challenge to keep them on track and keep them in the relationships they build up with clients. People need to know that they are doing a good job and that their work is valued.

With all the projects, staff, including volunteers, needed regular opportunities for support and supervision which would help them 'keep going'. Making time for this was important, but not always easy, particularly where staff or volunteers were working on a part-time sessional basis, as was the case with two projects. Individual projects varied in the extent to which they were able to meet these needs. Organisations which already prioritised supervision and training tended to be more successful in this respect.

One project developed a range of opportunities including fortnightly individual supervisions; staff and users get-togethers to prevent isolation; and staff meetings to discuss problems and successes, share information and have fun together. By making support more of a priority, earlier difficulties with retaining staff were much reduced.

One-to-one supervision sessions in this project provided a confidential space where people could talk openly about how they felt about participants and co-workers, about mistakes they felt they had made and about anything going on which might be affecting their work. They could test out ideas and get feedback on them and, last but not least, the sessions offered emotional support – having "someone there to back me up". However, they were very clear that these were "productive, work-based – not therapy – sessions!"

Support was often particularly valuable in the early days when staff and participants were getting to know one another and the fragile process of relationship building was getting underway.

> A and M are supporting Marsha, a young woman with high support needs. This relationship has required much supervision in group settings and individually due to Marsha's complex needs. Her workers now seem confident and reassured after a few weeks of feeling out of their depth and unsure.

In the employment project, starting a work placement was sometimes a point when both the participant and their support worker could feel particularly vulnerable and in need of support from a third party.

> We had got Paul a job on the production line of a factory where we felt the atmosphere would suit him. On his first day I was so nervous my heart was in my mouth. [The project manager] and myself supported him, but to be honest, she was there as much to support me as anything.

Not surprisingly, all the projects wanted to show that they had been successful – and they often were. Yet to some extent this was outside their control. Staff could facilitate to the best of their ability, but at the end of the day, factors over which they had no control might adversely influence the outcomes. In those circumstances project workers needed reassurance. Being part of a team where people could support one another informally was seen as important by some people, particularly by one person who had been working on her own until project funding meant that two more workers could be recruited.

In the case of one project, there was only one part-time worker and he found the lack of colleagues, and not being part of a team, difficult.

Project managers and leadership

The specific roles of the project managers were dictated by the aims of the individual projects, but there was a common task of 'holding it all together', particularly when projects ran into difficulties or there were setbacks. Managers had to be fully committed to what the project was seeking to achieve, but also be able to inspire and motivate staff they worked with. "I needed to be confident about the value and potential of the work."

Without this, it could be difficult to 'sell' the project to other people such as staff in other agencies and family carers. The project manager had the responsibility of holding things together and keeping the project afloat.

> As the manager, I conceived the original idea, co-ordinated the project and was responsible for support and supervision – and also for project development work, facilitating change and problem-solving, particularly in the first year. As well as administering the project, I also liased with houses and made the initial contacts in order to help with the difficult and time consuming parts of the work. I also needed to own the project and feel that it made sense to me as a manager. Workers were fighting hard but becoming demoralised. They might have left and the project would have folded. I had to pick things up when they were beginning to fall apart, find time to understand what was happening, while feeling pressurised to come up with results and outcomes.

The need for good project management was highlighted in one of the projects where the manager was no longer available. The impact of this was considerable. The actual work and the relationship with external agencies was disrupted temporarily until the new manager was established.

Managers in service systems often have little contact with service users, but this was not the case with the Choice Initiative projects. All the managers were involved in some 'hands-on' work with individual participants, either on a one-to-one basis or as a co-worker with one of the project staff. Although this took time away from project management it did, as one person put it, "help to make sense of the project".

Training

> We have a responsibility to train ourselves [so that we] bring always greater and more developed skills to the process.

As Tony Phillips' introduction to this chapter suggests, training for staff working in a truly person-centred and empowering way with people with high support needs is, with the exception of supported employment, in its infancy.

Some in house training took place within individual projects. For example, at Markfield a range of areas were covered: health and safety; emergency procedures; medical issues; communication skills, including signing, mirroring and using objects of reference; facilitation skills; advocacy skills; choice-making; good practice in personal care; working with carers; challenging behaviour; working with the public; turn-taking skills; how to access the community; minibus driving; training and assessment. Some of the training was experiential and involved discussion of values.

An in–house training day at Choices on communication (Anna Cheetham)

We started with a role-play using non-verbal communication. Staff were very concerned that as an interpreter or 'receiver' they might force the other person into doing something 'wrong' because rather than doing nothing, you feel you have to act. Through exercises and discussions we discovered that staff are very aware of how they are personally affected when they can't seem to interpret clients' vocalisations or expressions. When staff thought they were not 'getting it right' they identified feeling scared, defensive, impatient, uninterested, unconfident and withdrawn. Importantly however, workers did feel that on the occasions when they got it right they felt fulfilled by the experience.

We focused very much on what workers actively do to respond to their clients effectively. Staff reported that they recognised the following communicative acts: eye contact, smiles and other facial expressions, sounds, posture and movements. These subtle behaviours formed the basis for their interactions and decision-making. I felt glad that staff were aware of this and concerned about [these issues] as it proved their integrity and real concern for their clients.

Spending a day together helped workers realise that they were not alone with their fears, gave everyone a boost of confidence and enthusiasm for what can be achieved.

The Foundation also ran workshops for project staff on monitoring and evaluation, two workshops on communication and two on choice, the latter two highlighting the key themes in the Initiative. Project staff also received some training on presentation skills before the *Communication Matters* conference. Although these events included a teaching element, the overall approach was experiential learning.

Workshop on Choice led by Mandy Neville (Joe Nolan, Step Out)

The workshop was held a year after the projects had started and we met with feelings of achievement, mingled with expectations about the future. We had all experienced problems which we had sought to turn into the chance to thrive and develop.

Mandy Neville started by inviting each of us to describe a time in our lives when we had made a decision which had affected who we are today. The choices we'd made had varying degrees of significance but what became clear was our ability to exercise choice in our own lives.

...Mandy described her experiences with circles of support whose members are dedicated to acting on choices made by the person who is the focus of the circle. To illustrate the importance of circles, Mandy showed us a relationship map, highlighting how, for many people with learning disabilities, most of the people on that map would be professionals.

We then moved on to look at PATH, a person-centred planning tool which revealed how a person's dreams can become reality because PATH is a platform which enables people to express their wishes.

Mandy moving illustrated how a circle of support, together with person-centred planning can make a difference. We heard about how a young woman who does not use speech and is said to display 'challenging behaviour' was able to realise her dream of going to an ordinary school, has been to America and now plans to become a journalist.

In the afternoon, two participants volunteered to share a particular problem they were experiencing in their project. We divided into two groups, each with a speaker, a timekeeper and an information gatherer, the others being listeners or advisers. The speaker had six minutes to present their problem after which they were not allowed to speak. The listeners/advisers then had six minutes to give as much advice as possible.

My group had a lot of fun. Sticking to the general tenor of the day which was about 'dreaming', we were given licence to think as imaginatively as possible in order to generate possible solutions. Many of our ideas were downright outlandish but we were also able to offer some workable advice.

Mandy's presentation boosted our individual and collective enthusiasm and energy. By the end of the day, problems and difficulties were taking up a little less of our attention and our minds were more focused on workable ways of turning our ideas into reality.
(Foundation for People with Learning Disabilities, 1999)

Conclusion

For staff supporting people with learning disabilities, training has tended to be largely skills-based, often focusing on practical aspects of care. As the Choice Initiative projects demonstrated, this was sometimes important, but 'training' needed to be much broader.

Staff were challenged to think in depth about the values which underpinned their work: what is the real meaning of choice, for example? How do they try and ensure that they are really respecting a person's choice and not imposing their own ideas? How do you really get to know someone — and enable them to get to know you?

As the projects discovered, if people with high support needs are to find ways of making real choices, this requires a considerable degree of involvement from those supporting them. This, in turn, has implications for staffing levels.

Ongoing and regular opportunities for supervision and support were also crucial for staff who were often working intensively on a one-to-one basis and needing to draw on their own resource – to use themselves in the work. This could be very challenging, but also very rewarding.

Department of Health (1998) *Modernising Social Services.* London: The Stationery Office.

Foundation for People with Learning Disabilities (1999) *The Choice Initiative: Bulletin 5.* London: Foundation for People with Learning Disabilities.

Open Training College Dublin (1996) *Diploma in Training and Education in Supported Employment.* Dublin: The Open Training College.

Open University in partnership with People First and Mencap (1996) *Learning Disability: Working as Equal People.* Milton Keynes: Open University.

Chapter 10

Reflections
from the Choice Initiative

CONCLUSION

The Choice Initiative was set up in the belief that people with learning disabilities and high support needs have the right to play their part as full citizens. For this to happen,

> they need people attuned to listening to what they are saying without words and a huge amount of support alongside a wide range of opportunities.
> *(Mental Health Foundation, 1996:103)*

During the past two and a half years, we have developed our vision of a future where people with high support needs are able to take more control over their lives and decide on what they would like to do and how they would wish to live. We have been encouraged by the imagination, resourcefulness and determination of all those who have participated.

We believe that continuing progress depends on entitlement to support and services that promote choice and social inclusion.

For everyday lives, everyday choices, each person with learning disabilities and high support needs should have the right to

- communicate in a way that is appropriate to them

- be presented with a range of choices that are appropriate for them

- make choices about how they spend their days

- make choices about where they live and with whom

- have the opportunity to make friendships and relationships

- have their friendships and relationships respected

- be involved in risk assessment procedures that address both empowerment and protection

- have an advocacy partner if they so wish

- have sufficient staff to lead a full life in the community

- choose staff who value and respect their autonomy

- have access to transport to enable them to participate in the community

- have sufficient financial resources, including the opportunity to have Direct Payments if they so wish

- have their cultural, religious and ethnic backgrounds respected.

The impact of choice

The work in the projects has demonstrated that people can benefit from making choices in areas such as how they spend their time and how they live.

> Clients have shown greater happiness in their lives, just through this one day support.

> It's meant so much to people and changed different things in their lives and changed how they see themselves within the community.

As John O'Brien has said in the introduction, "these projects demonstrate that many people with substantial disabilities respond to project workers' interest in knowing them, accepting direction from them, and walking with them to open new possibilities".

The importance of communication partnerships

The key to the Choice Initiative has been the relationships that have been established over time between the participants and the project staff. Communication, if it is to be positive and meaningful, has to be based on trust. To have the appropriate tools is only part of the story. In some cases, gestures and facial expression alone have been the only clues to participants' wishes. Often others close to the person have also offered insights. There has been soul searching about the reality of people's choices and the most appropriate ways to enable each individual to make meaningful decisions.

> It really is getting to know the person, getting to know their carers and their families – and then just trying to build up a picture of what they enjoy and trying to extend what they are already doing... handing choice over gradually and finding people's levels.

> It's a fine line to make sure that the support workers are not influencing choice too much.

Support workers also have needed to assist participants to transform their wishes into reality, so that they would be motivated to communicate as they saw results.

Project workers have found real satisfaction in seeing the way participants' lives have been enriched.

> If you want this, if this is really what you want, then you can and I would like to be there to help you.

> We've wanted to open doors for people.

Support for staff

In trying to help others to capture their dreams, project workers have also needed support, through appropriate training, often based on experiential learning and exploring values.

> It's been really good to talk about our experiences. We've all shared the same things really.

They have valued sympathetic line managers who have been prepared to work alongside them, as well as helping them to explore the issues the work in the projects has raised.

Risk

In particular, it has been necessary to be sensitive to the risks involved in promoting choice and awareness of the duty of care. The Choice Initiative has shown that there are emotional as well as physical risks. One or two people have turned their back on choices they have made. This is a not unusual experience, but it does also serve as a reminder that some choices may need to be introduced after great thought and preparation, and that they may not always turn out as expected. The risks associated with choice need to be fully understood and accepted. Citizen advocates can play a key role in supporting their partners to make appropriate changes they would wish to bring to their lives.

Friendships

Choices do not always need to involve intense activity:

> She enjoys being round people, having a cup of tea, spending a long time sitting and watching people.

Interwoven in the life of the Choices projects was the importance of friendships. The Choice Initiative has shown that there needs to be wider acknowledgement of, and respect for, the importance of supporting people with high support needs to make and sustain ordinary friendships.

Obstacles to choice

Support staff have also experienced sadness and frustration at the restrictions many people with high support needs experience, for example, because of poverty, lack of transport, insufficient staffing, unsympathetic employers and inadequate support to family carers.

> We've lost clients who were initially involved in the project through lack of resources, through changes in staff.

> I think the main obstacle is a general attitude of society. Giving people access to mainstream facilities including people in all society's activities is not a general attitude.

Future challenges

There are real challenges if choice is to become the reality in the lives of people with learning disabilities and high support needs. Some practices will need to change, but above all, there needs to be acknowledgement that people's wishes should be sought and respected. For all who seek to find ways to empower people with high support needs, intuition and empathy are important alongside analytical skills. Roger Deacon, Head of Adult Services, Surrey County Council, Social Services Department has written in an unpublished document:

> *[There is] the need for us all (ie all stakeholders) to expand our imagination. Imagination is the key to creating opportunities, achievement and realisation. Often it is our lack of imagination that restricts our/people's belief in what people with learning disabilities and high support needs are capable of communicating and achieving.*

RECOMMENDATIONS

For everyday lives, everyday choices

The Foundation welcomes the opportunities afforded by the development of policies across government departments to enhance the life chances of people with learning disabilities and to facilitate social inclusion.

For those with high support needs, the findings of the Choice Initiative have suggested that there should be wider recognition that their wishes can be discovered and respected.

We have selected the following specific recommendations which we believe will be of particular importance in enhancing the choices of people with high support needs.

For government

- Choices for people with severe learning disabilities will require effective advocacy. One important step could be to implement sections 1 and 2 of the Disabled Persons Act 1986.

- Plans should be made to increase the number of specialist staff, such as speech and language therapists, and there should be equity of provision, so that people can maximise their ability to communicate and lead full lives.

- Values about choice and empowerment as well as skills and knowledge should be an integral part of the training of the social care workforce. These should be reflected in care standards.

- Reform of the benefits system is needed to remove the disincentives to people with learning disabilities taking up work opportunities, and to ensure that those who do not work have an adequate income. This would enable individuals to make choices with regard to lifestyle.

- The rights of people with learning disabilities and high support needs should be a priority for the Disability Rights Commission.

For commissioners in Local Authorities and Health Authorities

There is a need to:

- Develop effective and practical ways of consulting people with high support needs and their family carers when planning services.

- Ensure that advocacy services are available, which are independent of providers.

- Consider how best to provide access to Direct Payments to those who wish to have them, to enable people with learning disabilities and high support needs to achieve greater choice in their lives.

- Ensure that agencies have procedures in place and sufficient staffing levels to listen to people's choices and provide opportunities.

For staff responsible for individual assessment

There is a need to:

- Check assessment systems to ensure that they focus on the individual – for example, by using person-centred planning.

- Present a range of options in the transition from school or college, including further education, training and supported employment.

- Recognise the potential of good transport provision to improve quality of life and choice.

For service providers

There is a need to:

- Assess the communication needs of each individual and ensure that staff communicate appropriately. The development of a Communication Passport, for example, could facilitate this.

- Support actively individuals to make and sustain friendships and to encourage, for example, the setting up of a circle of support if the person wishes.

- Ensure that risk policies and procedures create a balance between safety and the provision of opportunities.

- Develop human resources policies and practices which create a stable workforce, and enhance continuity of relationships for people with learning disabilities and high support needs.

- Work closely with family carers, respecting their role in the lives of many people with high support needs.

Mental Health Foundation (1996) *Building Expectations: Opportunities and Services for People with a Learning Disability.* London: Mental Health Foundation.

Also by Sam Usher:

ISBN: 978-1-78370-547-4

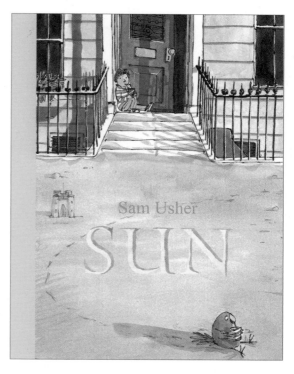

ISBN: 978-1-78370-795-9

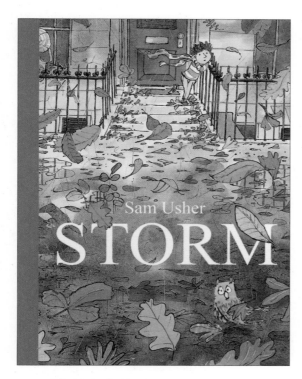

ISBN: 978-1-78741-242-2

ISBN: 978-1-78370-073-8

When we got back,
Grandad said,
"What a day!
You never know
what you're going
to find at the beach!"
And I said, "It was
brilliant – can we go
again tomorrow?"

Then we set sail for home.

We explored the shipwreck and the seals
showed us their pirate treasure.

And at last we got to have our swim.

"We did it!" I said.

"There's mum and dad!" said Grandad.

"Land ahoy!" I shouted.

"Ropes at the ready!"

"Hold tight!" said Grandad.

"Check the rigging!"

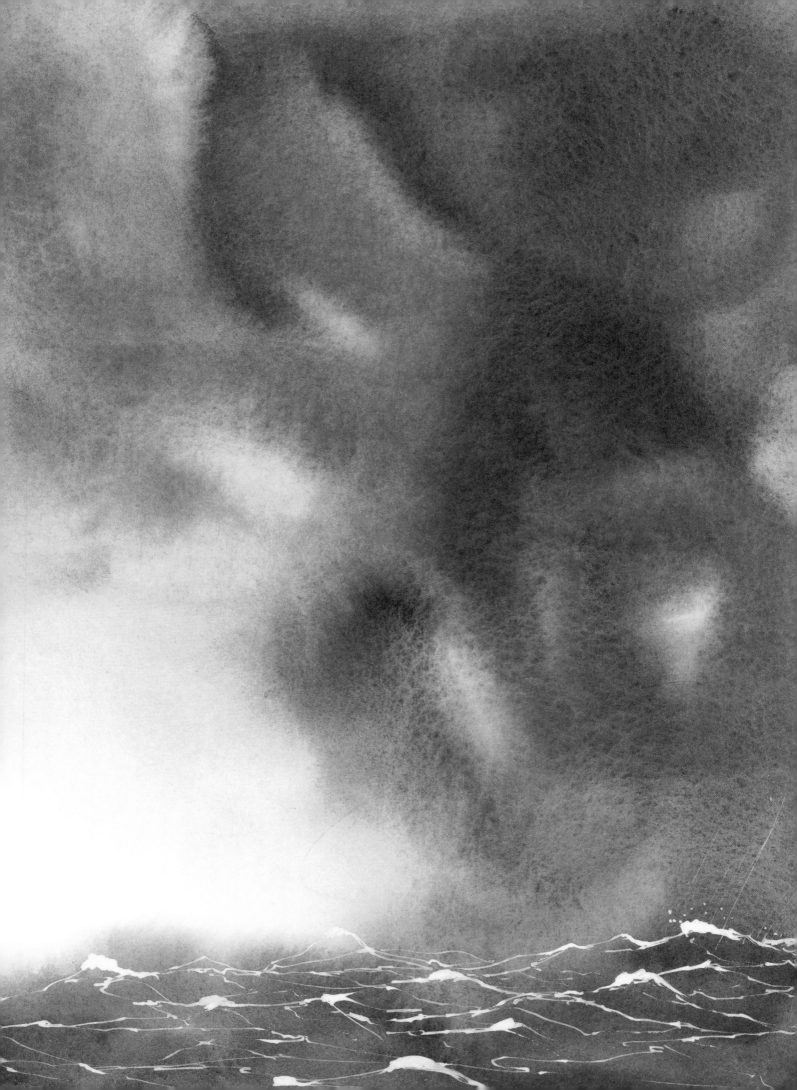